▴SCHOLASTIC

Weekly Reader:
SUMMER EXPRESS

New York • Toronto • London • Auckland • Sydney
Mexico City • New Delhi • Hong Kong • Buenos Aires

Editor: Ourania Papacharalambous
Cover design by Tannaz Fassihi and Michelle H. Kim
Interior design by Michelle H. Kim

ISBN: 978-1-338-10891-0
Compilation and illustrations copyright © 2017 by Scholastic Inc.
All rights reserved.
Printed in the U.S.A.
First printing, January 2017.

9 10   144   25 24

Table of Contents

Dear Parent,

Congratulations! You hold in your hands an exceptional educational tool that will give your child a head start in the coming school year.

Inside this book, you'll find 100 practice pages that will help your child review and learn reading and writing skills, grammar, place value, addition and subtraction, and so much more! *Weekly Reader: Summer Express* is divided into 10 weeks, with two practice pages for each day of the week, Monday through Friday. However, feel free to use the pages in any order that your child would like. Here are other features you'll find inside:

★ A weekly incentive chart and certificate to motivate and reward your child for his or her efforts.

★ A sheet of colorful stickers to use as weekly rewards.

★ Ideas for fun, skill-building activities you can do with your child any time.

★ Suggestions for creative learning activities that you can do with your child each week.

★ A certificate of completion to celebrate your child's accomplishments.

We hope you and your child will have a lot of fun as you work together to complete this workbook.

Enjoy!

The Editors

Tips for Using This Book

1. Pick a good time for your child to work on the activities. You may want to do it around mid-morning after play, or early afternoon when your child is not too tired.

2. Make sure your child has all the supplies he or she needs, such as pencils and an eraser. Designate a special place for your child to work.

3. Celebrate your child's accomplishments by letting him or her affix stickers to the incentive chart after completing the activities each day. Reward your child's efforts with a bonus sticker at the end of the week as well.

4. Encourage your child to complete the worksheets, but don't force the issue. While you may want to ensure that your child succeeds, it's also important that he or she maintains a positive and relaxed attitude toward school and learning.

5. After you've given your child a few minutes to look over the activity pages he or she will

be working on, ask your child to tell you his or her plan of action: "Tell me about what we're doing on these pages." Hearing the explanation aloud can provide you with insights into your child's thinking processes. Can he or she complete the work independently? With guidance? If your child needs support, try offering a choice about which family member might help. Giving your child a choice can help boost confidence and help him or her feel more ownership of the work to be done.

6. When your child has finished the workbook, present him or her with the certificate of completion on page 143. Feel free to frame or laminate the certificate and display it on the wall for everyone to see. Your child will be so proud!

Skill-Building Activities for Any Time

The following activities are designed to complement the 10 weeks of practice pages in this book. These activities don't take more than a few minutes to complete and are just a handful of ways in which you can enrich and enliven your child's learning. Use the activities to take advantage of time you might ordinarily disregard—for example, standing in line or waiting at a bus stop. You'll be working to practice key skills and have fun together at the same time.

Find Real-Life Connections

One of the reasons for schooling is to help children function in the real world, to empower them with the abilities they'll truly need. So why not put those developing skills into action by enlisting your child's help with creating a grocery list, reading street signs, sorting pocket change, and so on? He or she can apply reading, writing, science, and math skills in important and practical ways, connecting what he or she is learning with everyday tasks.

An Eye for Patterns

A red-brick sidewalk, a beaded necklace, a Sunday newspaper—all show evidence of structure and organization. You can help your child recognize the way things are structured, or organized, by observing and talking about patterns they see. Your child will apply his or her developing ability to spot patterns across all school subject areas, including attributes of shapes and solids (geometry) and characteristics of narrative stories (reading). Being able to notice patterns is a skill shared by effective readers and writers, scientists, and mathematicians.

Journals as Learning Tools

Most of us associate journal writing with reading comprehension, but having your child keep a journal can help you keep up with his or her developing skills in other academic areas as well—from telling time to matching rhymes. To get started, provide your child with several sheets of paper, folded in half, and stapled together. Explain that he or she will be writing and/or drawing in the journal to complement the practice pages completed each week. Encourage your child to draw or write about what he or she found easy, what was difficult, or what was fun. Before moving on to another set of practice pages, take a few minutes to read and discuss that week's journal entries together.

Promote Reading at Home

- Let your child catch you in the act of reading for pleasure, whether you like reading science fiction novels or do-it-yourself magazines. Store them someplace that encourages you to read in front of your child and **demonstrate that reading is an activity you enjoy.** For example, locate your reading materials on the coffee table instead of your nightstand.

- Set aside a family reading time. By designating a reading time each week, your family is assured an opportunity to discuss with each other what you're reading. You can, for example, share a funny quote from an article. Or your child can tell you his or her favorite part of a story. The key is to **make a family tradition of reading and sharing books** of all kinds together.

- **Put together collections of reading materials** your child can access easily. Gather them in baskets or bins that you can place in the family room, the car, and your child's bedroom. You can refresh your child's library by borrowing materials from your community's library, buying used books, or swapping books and magazines with friends and neighbors.

Skills Alignment

Listed below are the skills covered in the activities throughout *Weekly Reader: Summer Express*. These skills will help children review what they know while helping prevent summer learning loss. They will also better prepare each child to meet, in the coming school year, the math and language arts learning standards established by educators.

Math

	Week 1	Week 2	Week 3	Week 4	Week 5	Week 6	Week 7	Week 8	Week 9	Week 10
Solve addition and subtraction problems.	✦	✦	✦	✦	✦		✦	✦	✦	✦
Fluently add and subtract within 20.	✦	✦	✦	✦	✦					
Work with equal groups of objects to gain foundations for multiplication.	✦			✦						
Understand place value.			✦	✦				✦		
Use place value and properties of operations to add and subtract.	✦	✦	✦	✦	✦		✦		✦	✦
Measure and estimate lengths in standard units.		✦	✦	✦	✦	✦			✦	
Relate addition and subtraction to length.		✦			✦	✦				
Work with time and money.		✦		✦		✦	✦	✦	✦	
Represent and interpret data.			✦			✦	✦			✦
Reason with shapes and their attributes.		✦				✦	✦			

Language Arts

	Week 1	Week 2	Week 3	Week 4	Week 5	Week 6	Week 7	Week 8	Week 9	Week 10
Ask and answer questions about key details in a text.	✦	✦			✦	✦		✦	✦	✦
Identify the main topic or central message of a text.	✦	✦				✦		✦		✦
Describe characters, settings, and plot in a story.			✦		✦					
Describe connections within a text.				✦						
Describe the overall structure of a story.					✦					
Know and use text features.			✦			✦	✦	✦	✦	
Identify the main purpose of a text.								✦		✦
Use images and explain how they contribute to or help clarify a text.		✦		✦		✦				
Compare and contrast two texts.									✦	
Know and apply grade-level phonics and word analysis skills in decoding words.	✦	✦			✦	✦	✦	✦	✦	✦
Read with accuracy and fluency to support comprehension.	✦	✦	✦		✦	✦	✦			✦
Demonstrate command of the conventions of standard English grammar and usage.	✦	✦	✦	✦	✦		✦	✦		
Demonstrate command of the conventions of standard English capitalization, punctuation, and spelling when writing.	✦	✦		✦		✦		✦		
Use knowledge of language and its conventions when writing, speaking, reading, or listening.	✦	✦	✦	✦	✦	✦	✦	✦	✦	✦
Determine or clarify the meaning of unknown and multiple-meaning words and phrases.	✦	✦						✦	✦	✦
Demonstrate understanding of figurative language, word relationships, and nuances in word meanings			✦	✦	✦		✦			✦

Help Your Child Get Ready: Week 1

Here are some activities that you and your child might enjoy.

Sizzling Synonyms!

The first time your child says, "It's hot outside," challenge him or her to come up with as many words as possible that mean the same thing as *hot*. You can try this with other weather words such as *cold, rainy,* or *cloudy*.

Summer Goal

Suggest that your child come up with a plan to achieve a goal by the end of the summer. For example, he or she may wish to become an expert on a favorite animal or learn to count in another language. Help him or her map out a way to be successful. Periodically, check to see how your child is progressing.

Order, Order!

Play a ranking game. Choose three related items and ask your child to put them in order. Ask him or her to explain the choice. For example, if you chose *ice cube, snowball,* and *frozen lake*, your child might say *small, medium,* and *large; or cold, colder, coldest*.

Sun Safety

Talk about sun safety with your child. Ask him or her to write a list of ways to stay safe in the sun. Post it in a prominent place!

These are the skills your child will be working on this week.

Math

- skip-counting
- even and odd numbers
- subtraction

Reading

- main idea and details

Phonics & Vocabulary

- short vowels

Grammar & Writing

- collective nouns
- possessive nouns
- punctuation: statements
- sentence parts: nouns
- pronouns

Incentive Chart: Week 1

Week 1	Day 1	Day 2	Day 3	Day 4	Day 5
Put a sticker to show you completed each day's work.	☆ ☆	☆ ☆	☆ ☆	☆ ☆	☆ ☆

CONGRATULATIONS!

Wow! You did a great job this week!

This certificate is presented to:

_____

_____   _____
Date   Parent/Caregiver's Signature

A Group of Nouns

Nouns name people, places, and things. Special nouns name groups. These nouns are called collective nouns. A **collective noun** names a group of animals, people, or things.

Ants live together in a **colony**.

 A group of fish is called a **school**.

Bees travel together in a **swarm**.

 A group of people who are related to each other is a **family**.

A group of students who meet regularly to be taught is a **class**.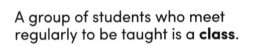

 People play sports together in a **team**.

Choose a word from the Word Bank to complete each sentence.

Word Bank					
colony	school	swarm	family	class	team

1 Our _____ will visit the science museum this fall.

2 The boat followed a _____ of fish.

3 My _____ volunteers at a soup kitchen every Thanksgiving.

4 I found a _____ of ants in our backyard.

5 Our school _____ won the soccer match!

6 Bees travel together in a _____ to find a new home.

Possessive Nouns

A **possessive noun** shows ownership. Add **'s** to make a singular noun show ownership. Add an **apostrophe** (') after the **s** of a plural noun to show ownership.

Underline the possessive noun in each sentence. Write S on the line if the possessive noun is singular. Write P if the possessive noun is plural.

1. Anna's family took a walk in the woods. _____

2. They saw two birds' nests high up in a tree. _____

3. A yellow butterfly landed on Brad's backpack. _____

4. Anna liked the pattern of the butterfly's wings. _____

5. A turtle's shell has many spots. _____

6. Anna took pictures of two raccoons' dens. _____

Complete each sentence with the singular possessive form of the noun in parentheses.

1. Jim wanted to play basketball at _____ house. (Carol)

2. One of _____ new sneakers was missing. (Jim)

3. He looked under his _____ desk. (sister)

4. He crawled under his _____ bed to look. (brother)

5. It was outside in his _____ flower garden. (dad)

6. Jim saw his _____ footprints in the dirt. (dog)

The Short List

Use the lines below to list words with the short /a/, /e/, /i/, /o/, and /u/ sounds. Choose words from the Word Bank.

Word Bank

bag	beg	bit	bog	dam
gas	gum	let	lip	met
box	mud	not	nut	pig

Short a _____ _____ _____

Short e _____ _____ _____

Short i _____ _____ _____

Short o _____ _____ _____

Short u _____ _____ _____

Choose a word from the Word Bank to rhyme with each underlined word.

Word Bank

bag	bin	lad	man
men	pig	Pop	us

1 A <u>tag</u> on the _____

2 <u>Ten</u> _____

3 A <u>big</u> _____

4 A <u>mad</u> _____

5 <u>In</u> the _____

6 A <u>bus</u> for _____

7 A <u>tan</u> _____

8 A <u>mop</u> for my _____

A Whale of a Sentence

A **statement**, or telling sentence, ends with a period (.).

Rewrite the sentences using capital letters and periods.

1 the blue whale is the largest whale in the world

_____

_____

2 blue whales are not part of the fish family

_____

_____

3 blue whales have no teeth

_____

4 blue whales eat tiny shrimp-like sea creatures called krill

_____

_____

5 blue whales have two blowholes

_____

_____

Who Did It?

A **noun**, or naming part of a sentence, can be a person.

Use the pictures to find naming parts to make each sentence complete. The first one is done for you.

1 *The skater* _____

skated on the ice.

2 _____

won the race.

3 _____

went inside the dark cave.

4 _____

climbed the wall.

5 _____

swam across the pool.

Skip Counting Caterpillars

Each of these caterpillars is skip counting by a different number. Can you figure out what each one is counting by? Fill in the numbers that they have missed.

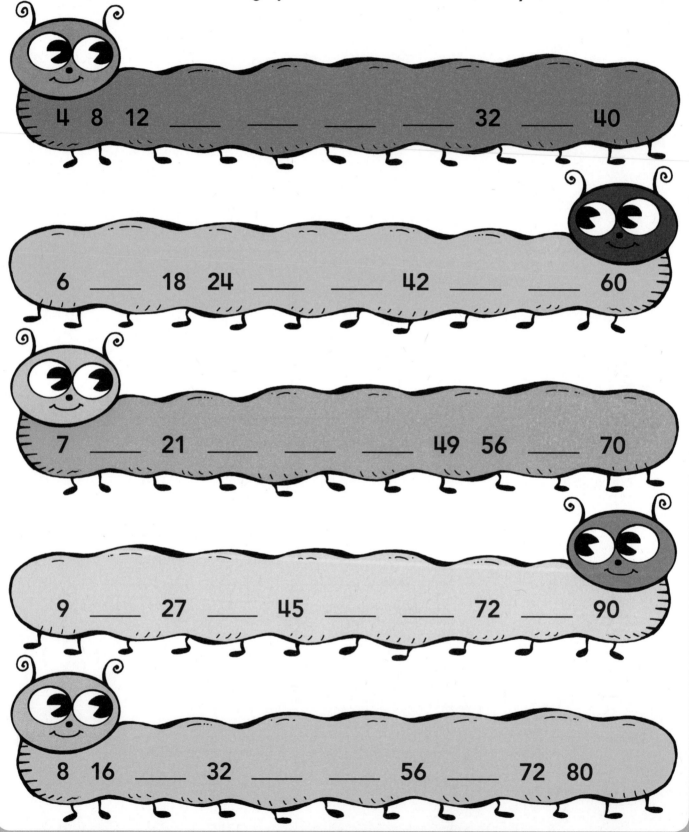

4   8   12   ___   ___   ___   32   ___   40

6   ___   18   24   ___   ___   42   ___   60

7   ___   21   ___   ___   ___   49   56   ___   70

9   ___   27   ___   45   ___   ___   72   ___   90

8   16   ___   32   ___   ___   56   ___   72   80

Send in the Subs

A **pronoun** is a word that can take the place of a noun.

Pronoun Substitutes					
he	you	we	they	it	she

The nouns in the sentences below need a rest.
Pick a pronoun to replace the underlined word(s).
Then write the sentence using the pronoun.

1 <u>Tanya</u> swings the bat.

_____

2 <u>Mr. Bartlet and Mr. Jones</u> blow their whistles.

_____

3 <u>Matt and I</u> warm up.

_____

4 <u>Leo</u> looks for his glove.

_____

5 <u>The ball</u> rolls into the field.

_____

6 <u>Jamal and I</u> cheer for the team.

_____

Frog in the Bog

Help! Frances the Frog is lost in the bog. Help her find her way home. Move one box at a time in any direction except diagonally. She can only hop on boxes that contain even numbers. And, of course, she doesn't want to stop on a box already occupied by a hungry alligator. Draw a line to show her path!

	6		3	5	7
9	4	2	8	13	75
47	11	1	44	24	19
21		36	12	17	15
23	43	18		35	27
25	21	32	20	22	26
51	29	27	45	68	53
33	89	37		42	
	31	Home Sweet Home	38	64	59

Courtney's Father

Read the story and answer the questions.

Courtney's father is a doctor. His name is Dr. Goodman. Everyone in our **community** thinks that he's a great doctor. I think so, too! Whenever I feel sick, my mother takes me to see him. He checks my temperature and asks me what is wrong. He always makes me feel much better.

Sometimes Courtney and I talk to her father about his work. He tells us that he had to study for a long time to become a doctor. He says that he is glad that he did because he loves to make people feel better. He showed us some of his books and explained to us how our hearts work. Courtney and I want to be doctors too when we get older.

1 What is the main idea of the story?

○ Courtney has a father.

○ Courtney's community has a great doctor.

○ Courtney is sick.

2 What is another word for **community**?

○ town   ○ country   ○ school

3 What does Dr. Goodman tell Courtney and the narrator about being a doctor?

_____

_____

4 How do the people in the town feel about Dr. Goodman?

_____

Sudoku Math

Every row, column, and 2-by-3 box should contain each of these digits in the answers:

1   **2**   **3**   **4**   **5**   **6**

Fill in each blank with the correct number to complete the fact.

$\begin{array}{r} 7 \\ -\ 6 \\ \hline \end{array}$	$\begin{array}{r} 15 \\ -\ \boxed{} \\ \hline 12 \end{array}$	$\begin{array}{r} 10 \\ -\ 5 \\ \hline \end{array}$	$\begin{array}{r} 13 \\ -\ 7 \\ \hline \end{array}$	$\begin{array}{r} 8 \\ -\ 4 \\ \hline \end{array}$	$\begin{array}{r} 9 \\ -\ 7 \\ \hline \end{array}$
$\begin{array}{r} \boxed{} \\ -\ 5 \\ \hline 1 \end{array}$	$\begin{array}{r} 12 \\ -\ 8 \\ \hline \end{array}$	$\begin{array}{r} 1\boxed{} \\ -\ 5 \\ \hline 7 \end{array}$	$\begin{array}{r} 11 \\ -\ 6 \\ \hline \end{array}$	$\begin{array}{r} 9 \\ -\ 6 \\ \hline \end{array}$	$\begin{array}{r} 1\boxed{} \\ -\ 3 \\ \hline 8 \end{array}$
$\begin{array}{r} 11 \\ -\ 7 \\ \hline \end{array}$	$\begin{array}{r} 8 \\ -\ 7 \\ \hline \end{array}$	$\begin{array}{r} 10 \\ -\ \boxed{} \\ \hline 7 \end{array}$	$\begin{array}{r} 8 \\ -\ 6 \\ \hline \end{array}$	$\begin{array}{r} 12 \\ -\ 6 \\ \hline \end{array}$	$\begin{array}{r} 12 \\ -\ 7 \\ \hline \end{array}$
$\begin{array}{r} 9 \\ -\ 4 \\ \hline \end{array}$	$\begin{array}{r} 1\boxed{} \\ -\ 7 \\ \hline 5 \end{array}$	$\begin{array}{r} 1\boxed{} \\ -\ 6 \\ \hline 10 \end{array}$	$\begin{array}{r} 1\boxed{} \\ -\ 5 \\ \hline 9 \end{array}$	$\begin{array}{r} 6 \\ -\ \boxed{} \\ \hline 5 \end{array}$	$\begin{array}{r} 1\boxed{} \\ -\ 5 \\ \hline 8 \end{array}$
$\begin{array}{r} 10 \\ -\ 7 \\ \hline \end{array}$	$\begin{array}{r} 8 \\ -\ 3 \\ \hline \end{array}$	$\begin{array}{r} 1\boxed{} \\ -\ 7 \\ \hline 7 \end{array}$	$\begin{array}{r} 1\boxed{} \\ -\ 8 \\ \hline 3 \end{array}$	$\begin{array}{r} 8 \\ -\ \boxed{} \\ \hline 6 \end{array}$	$\begin{array}{r} 10 \\ -\ 4 \\ \hline \end{array}$
$\begin{array}{r} 10 \\ -\ 8 \\ \hline \end{array}$	$\begin{array}{r} 14 \\ -\ 8 \\ \hline \end{array}$	$\begin{array}{r} 1\boxed{} \\ -\ 5 \\ \hline 6 \end{array}$	$\begin{array}{r} 1\boxed{} \\ -\ 8 \\ \hline 5 \end{array}$	$\begin{array}{r} 7 \\ -\ \boxed{} \\ \hline 2 \end{array}$	$\begin{array}{r} 10 \\ -\ 6 \\ \hline \end{array}$

Help Your Child Get Ready: Week 2

Here are some activities that you and your child might enjoy.

Scrambled Summer

Have your child write the words *summer vacation* on a sheet of paper and cut apart the letters. Encourage your child to use the letters to make new words. For variety, your child might also use the names of animals such as *elephant, alligator,* or *hippopotamus.*

Terrific Timelines

Help your child practice sequencing by creating timelines. For example, he or she can create a timeline of the daily routine. Encourage him or her to write sentences to describe what happens *first, next,* and so on. Challenge your child to create a timeline that includes the week's events, or one that shows at least one important event that occurred in each year of your child's life.

Rhyme Relay

Pick a word, such as *cat* or *dog,* to begin a rhyme relay. Take turns with your child saying words that rhyme with it.

Newspaper Scavenger Hunt

You can use a newspaper for many different scavenger hunts. For example, ask your child to find a certain number of proper nouns, adjectives, quotation marks, or exclamation points. Or, you may wish to challenge your child to find different parts of a newspaper, such as headlines, political cartoons, or captions.

These are the skills your child will be working on this week.

Math
- measure length
- use a number line to solve equations
- tell time
- add 2 digits without regrouping
- identify halves, thirds, and fourths

Reading
- reading comprehension

Phonics & Vocabulary
- long vowels

Grammar & Writing
- sentence parts: nouns
- irregular plurals
- sentence parts: verbs

Incentive Chart: Week 2

Week 2	Day 1	Day 2	Day 3	Day 4	Day 5
Put a sticker to show you completed each day's work.	☆ ☆	☆ ☆	☆ ☆	☆ ☆	☆ ☆

CONGRATULATIONS!

Wow! You did a great job this week!

This certificate is presented to:

_____

_____   _____
Date   Parent/Caregiver's Signature

A Walk in the Park

A **noun**, or the naming part of a sentence, can be a place or a thing.

Complete each sentence about the picture.
Use the nouns in the Word Bank below.

Word Bank

bench	bridge	carousel	children	stream	swing

1 The _____ is near the tree.

2 The _____ is beside the slide.

3 The _____ are playing in the park.

4 The _____ has six sections.

5 The _____ is over the stream.

6 The _____ runs through the park.

How Long Is It?

Use a ruler to measure each pencil. Measure from end to end.
Write the measurement below.

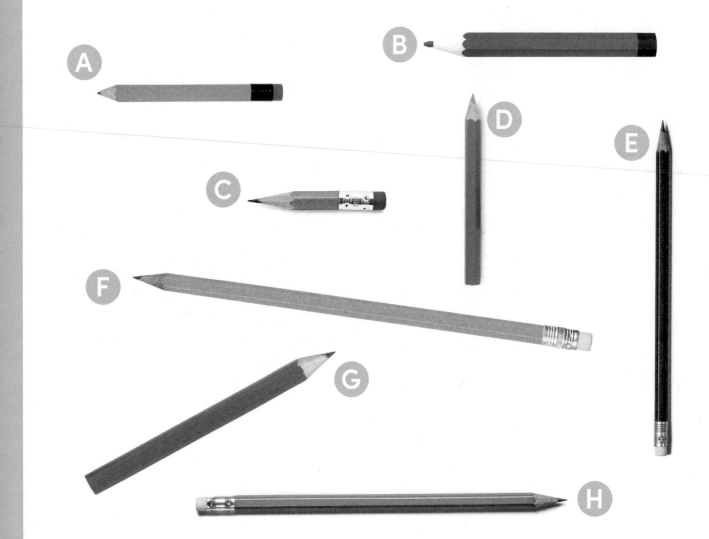

A _____ inches   E _____ inches

B _____ inches   F _____ inches

C _____ inches   G _____ inches

D _____ inches   H _____ inches

Irregular Plurals

Most plural nouns end in **s**.

1 bird   2 birds

Irregular plural nouns don't just add **s** to the singular to become plural.

1 child   2 children

Irregular plural nouns change their spellings in different ways. Some don't change at all.

> **Mice** are small rodents.
> **Geese** are large birds that make a honking sound.
> **Sheep** are animals whose fur is used for wool.
> Male **deer** have antlers.

Word Bank

children   dresses   feet   leaves   teeth   wolves

Write the plural for each word below. Use a word from the Word Bank.

1. tooth _____

2. child _____

3. foot _____

4. dress _____

5. leaf _____

6. wolf _____

Write the plural for each animal pictured below.

1 _____

3 _____

2 _____

4 _____

Use a Number Line

Complete each equation. Use the number line below.

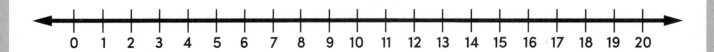

1 $2 + \boxed{} = 14$ **6** $6 + \boxed{} = 9$ **11** $5 + \boxed{} = 18$

2 $\boxed{} + 9 = 18$ **7** $\boxed{} + 11 = 16$ **12** $\boxed{} + 5 = 12$

3 $11 + 7 = \boxed{}$ **8** $14 + 3 = \boxed{}$ **13** $15 - 11 = \boxed{}$

4 $12 - \boxed{} = 9$ **9** $14 - \boxed{} = 2$ **14** $20 - \boxed{} = 4$

5 $19 - \boxed{} = 14$ **10** $12 - \boxed{} = 8$ **15** $11 - \boxed{} = 4$

A Snail's Pace

Long-vowel sounds can be spelled in different ways.
Some of the common spellings for long-vowel sounds are:

Long *a*	Long *e*	Long *i*	Long *o*
a_e	e_e	i_e	o_e
ai, ay	ea, ee	y, igh	oa, ow, oe

Read and write each word on the lines below.
Then organize the words by their long-vowel sounds.

1 deep _____

2 hole _____

3 toe _____

4 ride _____

5 meal _____

6 fly _____

7 snail _____

8 blow _____

9 here _____

10 game _____

11 lay _____

12 goat _____

13 might _____

14 these _____

long-*a* sound

_____

_____

_____

long-*i* sound

_____

_____

_____

long-*e* sound

_____

_____

_____

_____

long-*o* sound

_____

_____

_____

_____

Prime Timer

Write the time 2 ways.    Example: 1:15
15 minutes after 1

1

_____

_____ minutes to _____

4

_____

_____ minutes to _____

2

_____

_____ minutes after _____

5

_____

_____ minutes after _____

3

_____

_____ minutes to _____

6

_____

_____ minutes after _____

What's the Action?

The action part of a sentence is called a **verb**.
Example: *Chet **walks** to school every day.*

Look at each picture.
Then, complete each sentence about the picture using an action word, or verb.
Remember to use correct punctuation.

1 Mr. Downs _____

_____

3 James _____

_____

2 The fish _____

_____

4 Cara _____

_____

Write three sentences describing how you get ready in the morning.
Use a verb in each.

1 _____

2 _____

3 _____

What does a teapot do when it is mad?

Add. Solve the riddle using your answers.

21 + 14 ___ **N**	12 + 15 ___ **I**	20 + 19 ___ **U**	14 + 14 ___ **W**	23 + 31 ___ **P**	35 + 13 ___ **T**
11 + 13 ___ **L**	44 + 12 ___ **S**	21 + 43 ___ **B**	26 + 21 ___ **R**	50 + 18 ___ **O**	26 + 53 ___ **E**

Solve the Riddle!

Write the letter that goes with each number.

___ ___   ___ ___ ___ ___ ___
27   48   64   24   68   28   56

___ ___ ___   ___ ___ ___
27   48   56   48   68   54

Abraham Lincoln

Read the article. Then answer the questions.

Abraham Lincoln was the 16th President of the United States. When he was a boy, his family lived in a small log **cabin**. It had only one room and only one window. The walls were made from stacked-up tree logs. It had a dirt floor.

There was no electricity then. So, Abe's family got light from candles and the fireplace. Abe loved to read books by candlelight. One of his favorite books was about George Washington!

When Abraham Lincoln grew up, he became a lawyer. Then in 1861, he became President of the United States.

Abe grew up in a home just like this one. He helped to chop wood outside the cabin.

1. Which of these means almost the same thing as **cabin**?
   - ○ small house
   - ○ castle
   - ○ large house

2. What is this article about?
   - ○ the White House
   - ○ George Washington
   - ○ Abraham Lincoln

3. What job did Abraham Lincoln have before he became president?
   - ○ teacher
   - ○ candle maker
   - ○ lawyer

4. Which of these did Abe do inside the cabin?
   - ○ read books
   - ○ chop wood
   - ○ wash windows

Challenge

Why do you think it was dark inside the cabin?

_____

_____

Parts of a Shape

Each shape has been divided into equal parts. Below each shape, write whether that shape is divided into two halves, three thirds, or four fourths.

1

_____

2

_____

3

_____

4

_____

5

_____

6

_____

7

_____

8

_____

9

_____

10

_____

Help Your Child Get Ready: Week 3

Here are some activities that you and your child might enjoy.

What's Your Estimate?

Ask your child to estimate how many times in 60 seconds he or she can say "Mississippi" or write his or her name. Then have him or her try each activity and compare the results with the estimate.

Words Can Add Up

Assign a monetary value to words. For example, a consonant can be worth one penny and a vowel can be worth one nickel. Challenge your child to find a word with a high value.

Room With a View

Invite your child to look out of a window. Have your child describe or draw ten things in the scene. Remind your child to use lots of detail.

Silly Summer Sentences

How can summer turn into a tongue twister? Guide your child to make up a sentence using the word *summer* and as many other words as possible that start with the letter *s*.

These are the skills your child will be working on this week.

Math
- understand comparison symbols
- addition
- subtraction
- estimate length
- add and subtract 10
- number patterns

Reading
- identify key details
- read a glossary

Grammar & Writing
- use adjectives
- irregular verbs
- reflexive pronouns
- synonyms

Incentive Chart: Week 3

Week 3	Day 1	Day 2	Day 3	Day 4	Day 5
Put a sticker to show you completed each day's work.	☆ ☆	☆ ☆	☆ ☆	☆ ☆	☆ ☆

CONGRATULATIONS!

Wow! You did a great job this week!

This certificate is presented to:

_____

_____   _____
Date   Parent/Caregiver's Signature

Adjectives

An **adjective** is a word that describes a person, place, or thing.

Read each sentence.
Write the adjective that describes the underlined noun.

1 We live near a sparkling <u>brook</u>.   _____

2 It has clear <u>water</u>.   _____

3 Large <u>fish</u> swim in the brook.   _____

4 Busy <u>squirrels</u> play near the brook.   _____

5 You can enjoy breathing in the
fresh <u>air</u> near the brook.   _____

Complete each sentence by adding an adjective.

1 I love _____ apples.

2 I see a _____ ball.

3 I smell _____ flowers.

4 I hear _____ music.

5 I like _____ grapes.

Write three sentences that tell about the foods you like the best.
Use adjectives in your description.

_____

_____

_____

Symbols of Comparison

Rewrite each statement. Use the symbols <, >, or =.
The first one is done for you.

1 5 is greater than 2

$$5 > 2$$

7 7 is equal to 7

_____

2 2 is less than 3

_____

8 9 is less than 10

_____

3 8 is greater than 1

_____

9 5 is equal to 5

_____

4 19 is less than 23

_____

10 98 is greater than 52

_____

5 74 is greater than 73

_____

11 200 is less than 201

_____

6 56 is equal to 56

_____

12 99 is less than 100

_____

Lunch Lady

by Karen Jackson

Karen Jackson wrote about someone she admires. Read what she wrote.

I don't know her name. She is one of the workers in our school cafeteria. I call her Lunch Lady. She's my friend. There are many nice ladies in the cafeteria, but the Lunch Lady is the nicest of all. Every day she smiles at me when I go through the line. She says things like, "Hi Karen! Are you having a good day?" Lunch Lady always remembers that I like chicken nuggets the best and says, "Look, your favorite!" One day, I tripped and dropped my tray. Food went all over the floor. I was so embarrassed, but Lunch Lady came to my rescue. She helped me pick up the mess and she told me, "Don't worry about it. It's okay." That made me feel better. Another time, I was at the shoe store with my mom, and I saw Lunch Lady. She gave me a big hug. The reason I admire Lunch Lady is because she is friendly and kind.

Read each sentence below. Find the words that are wrong and cross them out. Then above them write the correct word or words that make the sentence true.

1. Karen wrote about Lunch Man.

2. Karen's favorite food is hot dogs.

3. Lunch Lady frowns when Karen comes through the line.

4. When Karen dropped her tray, Miss Daniels helped her.

5. One time, Karen saw Lunch Lady at the hardware store.

6. Karen admires Lunch Lady because she is friendly and mean.

The Sign Snatcher

The sign snatcher has taken the plus and minus signs from each equation. Can you put the correct ones back in?

Example:

15 ☐ 5 ☐ 1 = 11 ➡ 15 ☐−☐ 5 ☐+☐ 1 = 11

Complete each equation. Put a plus or a minus sign in each of the boxes.

1.   5 ☐ 5 ☐ 10 = 20

2.   7 ☐ 2 ☐ 10 = 19

3.   8 ☐ 3 ☐ 5 = 10

4.   16 ☐ 1 ☐ 2 = 13

5.   100 ☐ 100 ☐ 50 = 50

6.   42 ☐ 4 ☐ 2 = 48

7.   78 ☐ 2 ☐ 10 = 70

Remember to check your answers by trying the equations after putting in the signs.

8.   5 ☐ 3 ☐ 12 = 14

Challenge

Try this even more challenging equation.

330 ☐ 110 ☐ 4 = 224

Riddle Fun

Most verbs are regular. Their past-tense form ends in **-ed**.
Some verbs are **irregular**. The past-tense form of irregular verbs does not end in **-ed**.

The chart below shows the present and past tense of some irregular verbs.

Irregular Verbs					
Present Tense	eat	grow	ride	sit	tell	write
Past Tense	ate	grew	rode	sat	told	wrote

**Read each riddle. Write the answer using
one of the past-tense verbs from the box.
Write a complete sentence.**

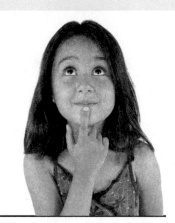

1 I sat on the seat and pushed the pedals with my feet.
I went from my house to the park. What did I do?

I_____

2 I was shorter and weighed less last year.
My clothes were smaller, too. What did I do?

I_____

3 I used my knife and fork.
Soon my plate was empty. What did I do?

I_____

4 I got out some paper and a pen.
I thought about what to tell my friend. What did I do?

I_____

5 I took a seat and waited.
I stayed in the chair until it was my turn. What did I do?

I_____

How Long Is It?

Estimate the length of each ribbon in centimeters (cm).
Use a ruler to check your estimate. Write your answers.

	Estimate	**Actual**
1	_____ cm	_____ cm
2	_____ cm	_____ cm
3	_____ cm	_____ cm
4	_____ cm	_____ cm
5	_____ cm	_____ cm
6	_____ cm	_____ cm

Cut a 14-centimeter length of paper into three pieces.
On the dots below, tape the pieces from shortest to longest.
Measure and write the length of each piece of paper.

• _____ cm

• _____ cm

• _____ cm

Flex Yourself

A **pronoun** takes the place of a noun in a sentence. A **reflexive pronoun** is a special kind of pronoun. Reflexive pronouns point back to the subject of the sentence.

Singular reflexive pronouns end in **-self.** Plural reflexive pronouns end in **-selves.**

Reflexive Pronouns	
Singular	**Plural**
myself	ourselves
yourself	yourselves
himself, herself, itself	themselves

Circle the reflexive pronoun in each sentence.
Then draw a line to the subject it points back to.
The first one is done for you.

1 The dog saw (itself) in the mirror

2 We trust ourselves to do the right thing.

3 Janet blamed herself for the mistake.

4 I washed the car myself.

5 You need to take care of yourself.

6 Jake and Alice will fix the house themselves.

7 Peter talks to himself.

8 You children should treat yourselves to an iced tea.

Add and Subtract

Above each number, write the number that is 10 more.
Below each number, write the number that is 10 less.
The first one is done for you.

1 | 68 | 58 | 48

1 68 / 58 / 48

5 27

9 83

2 19

6 44

10 50

3 75

7 39

11 89

4 31

8 62

12 48

Science Glossary

A glossary gives the meanings of difficult words in a book. Read the glossary words below. Then fill in the bubbles for the words that mean the same as the underlined words.

adaptation (ad-ap-TAY-shun) something an animal has that helps it stay alive. A giraffe's long neck is an adaptation that helps it eat leaves high in trees.

coating (KOHT-ing) a layer that covers something

hail (hayl) balls of ice that fall from the sky

precipitation (prih-sip-ih-TAY-shun) water falling from the sky as rain, snow, hail, or sleet

shelter (SHEL-tur) a place where someone or something is safe and protected

survive (sur-VIV) to stay alive

1 The butterfly used the large leaf as <u>a place to stay safe</u> during the storm.

  ○ coating   ○ precipitation   ○ shelter

2 <u>Balls of ice falling from the sky</u> can break car windows.

  ○ Adaptation   ○ Survive   ○ Hail

3 Desert animals can <u>stay alive</u> for a long time without water.

  ○ survive   ○ precipitation   ○ shelter

4 An ant's waterproof body is one <u>thing that helps it stay alive.</u>

  ○ precipitation   ○ adaptation   ○ shelter

5 During a rainstorm, insects can get covered with <u>water falling from the sky.</u>

  ○ coating   ○ precipitation   ○ shelter

Number-Pattern Parades

Figure out the pattern for each of these series.
What number comes next? Fill in the next number in the box at the end.

1 20   40   60   80   100   120   140   160   180   ☐

2 4   40   400   4,000   40,000   ☐

3 1   2   2   3   3   3   4   4   4   4   5   5   5   5   ☐

4 21   12   32   23   43   34   54   ☐

5 33 – 11 = 22   32 – 10 = 22   31 – 9 = 22   ☐

6 14 + 5 = 19   13 + 6 = 19   12 + 7 = 19   ☐

Challenge

What comes next in each of these patterns?

EXAMPLE: 3   1   4   2   5   3   6
              -2   +3   -2   +3   -2   +3

A 1   2   4   7   11   16   ☐

B 3   2   6   5   9   8   12   11   ☐

 Look at the relationship between each number and the number that follows it in the series.

Help Your Child Get Ready: Week 4

Here are some activities that you and your child might enjoy.

Compound Interest

Point out examples of compound words to your child. Then have him or her keep track of the compound words heard during an hour. Try it another time and challenge your child to improve on his or her last "score."

Start Collecting

Having a collection is a great way for a child to develop higher-level thinking skills such as sorting and analyzing. Encourage your child to start one. Leaves, rocks, stamps, or shells are all easy and fun things to collect. Your child can also practice comparing and contrasting by discussing how the items in his or her collection are similar and different.

The Case of the Mysterious Sock

Invite your child to find a secret object to put in a sock. Try to guess what it is by feeling the object through the sock. Trade roles. Play again.

Pet Autobiography

Suggest that your child write the story of your pet's (or an imaginary pet's) life. The story should be an autobiography— told from the pet's point of view!

These are the skills your child will be working on this week.

Math

- addition
- tell time
- write addition expressions using arrays
- estimate and measure lengths
- write numbers in expanded form
- add 2 digits with regrouping

Reading

- sequence

Phonics & Vocabulary

- common letter patterns

Grammar & Writing

- use adverbs
- write adverbial phrases
- combine sentences

Incentive Chart: Week 4

Week 4	Day 1	Day 2	Day 3	Day 4	Day 5
Put a sticker to show you completed each day's work.	☆ ☆	☆ ☆	☆ ☆	☆ ☆	☆ ☆

CONGRATULATIONS!

Wow! You did a great job this week!

This certificate is presented to:

_____

_____   _____
Date   Parent/Caregiver's Signature

Adding Up Adverbs

An **adverb** is a word that tells how, when, or where an action takes place.

3	4	5	6	7	8	9	10	11	12	13	14	15	16	18	19	20
g	t	u	r	q	t	o	c	a	e	s	i	f	y	n	v	l

Add. Use the chart above to write letters on the blanks to spell adverbs.

____	____	____	____	____	____			
3 + 0	11 + 1	9 + 9	6 + 2	9 + 11	15 + 1			

____	____	____	____	____	____	____	____	
1 + 9	17 + 3	6 + 6	10 + 9	9 + 3	2 + 4	2 + 18	5 + 11	

____	____	____	____	____	____	____		
5 + 2	4 + 1	7 + 7	8 + 4	3 + 1	10 + 10	9 + 7		

____	____	____	____	____	____	____	____	____	____
8 + 2	5 + 6	3 + 2	5 + 3	10 + 4	7 + 2	1 + 4	6 + 7	12 + 8	8 + 8

____	____	____	____	____	____	____	____	____	____
2 + 1	3 + 3	7 + 4	5 + 5	7 + 5	8 + 7	5 + 0	15 + 5	11 + 9	9 + 7

Complete each sentence with an adverb from above.

1 The ballerina danced _____ to the music.

2 The children crossed the street _____.

3 The cat _____ cleaned her new kittens.

4 The boy read his book _____ at the library.

5 The detective _____ solved the mystery.

Solving for Elapsed Time: Hours

Write the times shown on the left and on the right.
Then match each time on the left with the correct clock on the right.

LEFT	**RIGHT**

1 Fours hours after 6:00 =

A  =

2 Two hours after 2:00 =

B  =

3 Two hours before 2:00 =

C  =

4 Seven hours after 1:00 =

D  =

5 One hour before 7:00 =

E  =

6 Six hours after 3:00 =

F =

Challenge

Shania went to the beach at 10:00 A.M. and stayed for six hours.

What time did she leave the beach? _____

Circle the answers that match above.

Chugging Along

Write an ending for each sentence that tells where or when the action takes place.

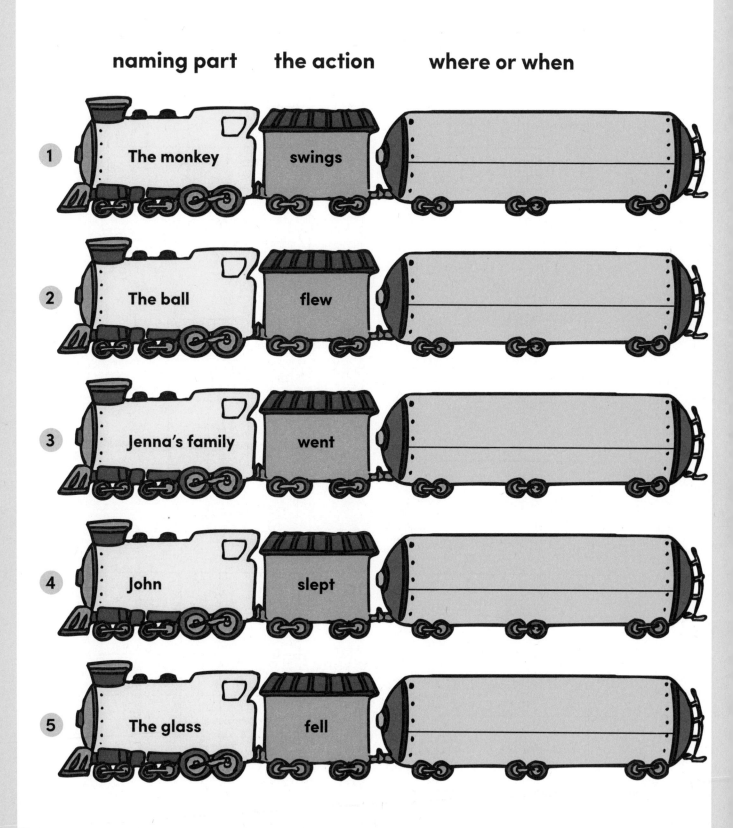

naming part   the action   where or when

1 The monkey   swings

2 The ball   flew

3 Jenna's family   went

4 John   slept

5 The glass   fell

Use an Array to Add

Number each array of squares to find the total.
Then write an equation that shows the total as the sum of equal addends.
The first one is done for you.

1

1	2	3	4
5	6	7	8
9	10	11	12

12 = 3 + 3 + 3 + 3

4

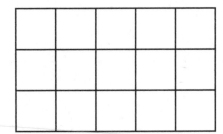

_____

2

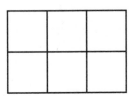

_____

5

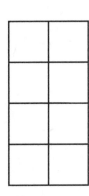

_____

3

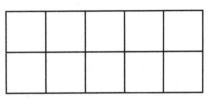

_____

6

_____

Ketchup and Mustard

Sometimes two sentences can be combined to make one sentence.

Sentences that share the same subject go together like ketchup and mustard. Rewrite the sentences by combining their endings with the word *and*.

1 I ordered eggs. I ordered hash browns.

I ordered eggs and hash browns.

2 I like onions on my hash browns. I like ketchup on my hash browns.

_____

_____

3 My mom makes great apple pie. My mom makes great applesauce.

_____

_____

4 My dad eats two helpings of meat loaf! My dad eats two helpings of potatoes!

_____

_____

5 My brother helps set the table. My brother helps clean the dishes.

_____

_____

6 We have berries for dessert. We have ice cream for dessert.

_____

Measuring Up

Look at each picture. Estimate how long you think it is. Then measure each picture with a ruler. Write the actual length in centimeters.

Estimate   **Actual**

1      _____ cm   _____ cm

2   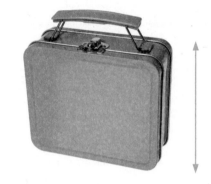   _____ cm   _____ cm

3      _____ cm   _____ cm

4   _____ cm   _____ cm

Twinkle, Twinkle

These letters commonly join together to make their own sound.

ank → sank   ink → sink   ing → sing   ong → song

Read and write each word on the lines below.
Then organize the words by their spellings.

1 twinkle _____

2 thank _____

3 along _____

4 bring _____

5 drank _____

6 think _____

7 strong _____

8 ankle _____

9 belong _____

10 string _____

11 drink _____

12 nothing _____

ank

_____

_____

_____

ink

_____

_____

_____

ing

_____

_____

_____

ong

_____

_____

_____

Find three pairs of words that have identical spellings except for one letter.

_____   _____   _____

_____   _____   _____

Expanding Numbers

Write each number in expanded form.
The first one is done for you.

1 57 = _50 + 7_____

2 23 = _____

3 61 = _____

4 86 = _____

5 14 = _____

6 99 = _____

7 325 = _____

8 469 = _____

9 743 = _____

10 872 = _____

11 162 = _____

12 984 = _____

A Pencil Sandwich

Read the passage about how pencils are made.

How does the lead get inside a wooden pencil? Pencils are made out of strips of wood cut from cedar trees. Then, grooves are cut in the strips. A mixture of graphite and clay is laid into the grooves. (We call it lead, but it is really a graphite mixture.) Then another strip of wood is glued on top of the first one, making a pencil sandwich! The wood is rounded in rows on the top strip of wood and the bottom strip. Then the pencils are cut apart and painted. An eraser is added on the end and held in place by a metal ring. When you buy a pencil, you sharpen it, and then you are ready to write.

Now, look at the pictures and their descriptions. Number each picture in the order that a pencil is made as described in the passage.

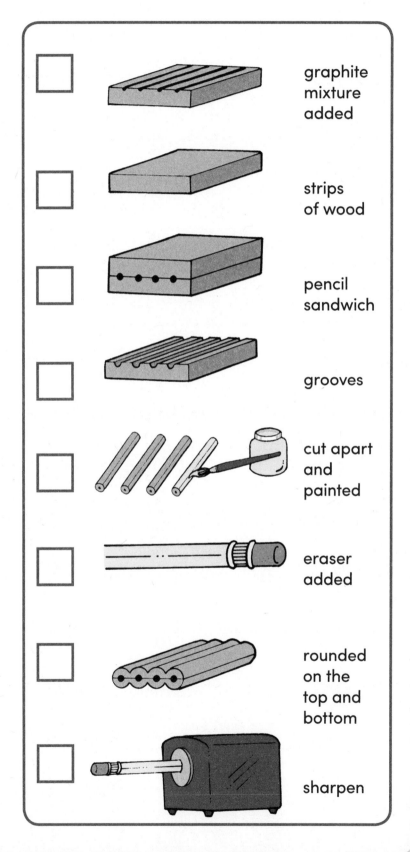

graphite mixture added

strips of wood

pencil sandwich

grooves

cut apart and painted

eraser added

rounded on the top and bottom

sharpen

Nutty Math

Add. Then solve the riddle below using the code.

92	94	71	45	51	52	80	62
G	O	H	D	T	S	U	N

27	55	33	69	42	47	65	22	36
+18	+39	+47	+23	+29	+15	+15	+29	+16

___ ___   ___ ___   ___ ___   ___ ___   ___ ___   ___ ___   ___ ___   ___ ___   ___ ___

What kind of nuts have no shell and nothing inside?

_____

Add. Then solve the riddle below using the code.

55	64	34	71	28	50	82
N	L	A	S	U	W	T

21	17	38	16	19	56	45
+29	+17	+26	+39	+ 9	+26	+26

___ ___   ___ ___   ___ ___   ___ ___   ___ ___   ___ ___   ___ ___

What kind of nuts hang on the wall?

_____

Help Your Child Get Ready: Week 5

Here are some activities that you and your child might enjoy.

Carrot-Turnip-Pea

Develop your child's listening skills by playing "Word Chain." In this game, someone says a word, and the next person must say a word that begins with the last letter of the previous player's word.

Now You See It, Now You Don't

Show your child an interesting picture and ask him or her to look at it for a minute. Then turn the picture over and ask your child to list the objects in it that he or she can remember on a sheet of paper. If you wish, allow your child to look at the picture for another minute and then add more items to the list. For a twist, use a picture with less detail, but ask your child to list the words in alphabetical order.

Secret Messages

Suggest that your child come up with a code to write secret messages. Have him or her trade messages with you or another family member.

Can You Judge a Book by Its Cover?

Give your child a chance to create a new cover for a favorite book. Remind him or her to include the title, as well as the names of the author and any illustrator. Encourage your child to include an image or images that he or she thinks would inspire someone to read the book.

These are the skills your child will be working on this week.

Math
- addition
- subtraction
- multiplication
- add and subtract 2 digits with regrouping
- add measurements
- compare lengths

Reading
- make inferences

Phonics & Vocabulary
- short vowels

Grammar & Writing
- write 3-part sentences
- expand sentences with descriptive words
- parts of speech
- combine sentences

Incentive Chart: Week 5

Week 5	Day 1	Day 2	Day 3	Day 4	Day 5
Put a sticker to show you completed each day's work.	☆ ☆	☆ ☆	☆ ☆	☆ ☆	☆ ☆

CONGRATULATIONS!

Wow! You did a great job this week!

This certificate is presented to:

_____

_____   _____
Date   Parent/Caregiver's Signature

Short Vowels

If a word has one vowel between two consonants, the vowel usually has a short sound.

Short Vowels:

a in *fan*   e in *hen*   i in *wig*   o in *cot*   u in *rug*

Say the name of each picture. Write the correct vowel to complete the word.

1 v____n

2 c____p

3 f____x

4 h____t

5 j____t

6 b____d

7 r____t

8 h____t

9 f____n

10 r____d

Read the words in the Word Bank. Listen for the short-vowel sound.
Write each word in the correct column in the chart.

Word Bank

fed	rid	rut	fat	cog
jug	had	mug	rap	cod
kit	jot	wet	zip	yes

Short a	Short e	Short i	Short o	Short u
_____	_____	_____	_____	_____
_____	_____	_____	_____	_____
_____	_____	_____	_____	_____

How Many Is That?

To solve these problems, you need to provide the numbers.
Read the clues, figure out the numbers, and solve the problems.

1 Multiply the number of states in the United States by the number of horns

on a bull. What's the product? _____

2 Subtract the number of bases on a baseball field from the number of letters

in the alphabet. What's the difference? _____

3 Add the number of days in most years to the number of seasons.

What's the sum? _____

4 Subtract the number of arms on an octopus from the number of sides

on an octagon. What's the difference? _____

5 Multiply the number of children in a set of twins by the number of wheels

on a tricycle. What's the product? _____

6 Subtract the number of eggs in a dozen

from the number of hours in a day.

What's the difference? _____

Challenge

Multiply the number of legs on a snake by the number of states in the U.S.

What's the product? _____

Silly Sentences

A sentence may have three parts: **a naming part, an action,** and a part that tells **where or when**.

Complete each missing part to make silly sentences.

the naming part	the action	where or when
1 The monkey		on his head.
2 My dad	is hopping	
3	flipped	in the forest.
4	bounced	
5 My shoes		at the pool.
6 The snake	twisted	
7 The bubbles	filled	

Challenge

On another sheet of paper, write a new sentence by scrambling the three parts listed above. For example, use the naming part in #1, the action part in #2, and the where or when part from #3. Draw a picture of your sentence.

Teenie Tiny Babies

Add or subtract.

U   42
      + 39

L   53
      − 48

N   31
      + 29

C   74
      − 28

O   44
      + 46

P   75
      − 37

H   40
      − 17

K   27
      + 36

S   96
      − 48

A   62
      − 48

G   80
      − 62

M   55
      + 16

R   88
      − 19

Write the letter that goes with each number.

I am smaller than your
thumb when I'm born.

___ ___ ___ ___ ___ ___ ___ ___
63   14   60   18   14   69   90   90

I am even smaller.

___ ___ ___ ___ ___
63   90   14   5   14

I am smaller than
a bumblebee.

___ ___ ___ ___ ___ ___ ___
90   38   90   48   48   81   71

Since we are so little,
we live right next to our
mother in a safe warm

___ ___ ___ ___ ___ .
38   90   81   46   23

At the Beach

A **describing word** makes a sentence more interesting.

Read the describing words on each beach ball.
Add the describing words to each sentence to make them more interesting.
Write each new sentence.

1 The snow cone sat in the sun.

melting   bright

_____

_____

2 Many children ran toward the ocean waves.

excited   crashing

_____

_____

3 My friends built a sand castle.

new   large

_____

_____

4 Our dog tried to catch the beach ball.

playful   flying

_____

_____

Building a Boat

The story is missing some words and numbers. Fill in the blanks with the number, noun, verb, adjective, or other type of word listed below the blank. Then solve the problem below.

My class is building a boat. We have

named it the S.S. _____.
                        (noun)

We are using wood and _____.
                              (plural noun)

We plan to sail it on _____
                        (last name of a boy or girl)

Lake and possibly the _____
                          (last name of a boy or girl)

River. We need a lot of wood. _____ brought in a board that was
                                  (name of girl)

_____ inches long. _____ brought a board that was
(double-digit number   (name of a boy)
less than 50)

_____ inches long. That's all the wood we have so far, but we are
(double-digit number
from 13 to 49)

going to buy more. We are going to raise money by selling _____
                                                              (plural noun)

during lunch. I'm sure we'll make enough _____ money in no time!
                                              (adjective)

What is the combined length of the wood the boat builders have so far? Answer in feet and inches.

_____

Cake and Ice Cream

Two sentences that share the same subject can be combined to make one sentence by using the word *and*.

Rewrite the sentences by combining their endings.

1. The party was fun.
   The party was exciting.

The party was fun and exciting.

2. We blew up orange balloons.
   We blew up green balloons.

3. We ate cake.
   We ate ice cream.

4. The cake frosting was blue.
   The cake frosting was yellow.

5. We made a bookmark.
   We made a clay pot.

6. We brought games.
   We brought presents.

What do you call a swimmer who was at the scene of a crime?

Subtract. Solve the riddle using your answers below.

41 − 25 —— Y	22 − 19 —— W	74 − 16 —— F	51 − 34 —— N	62 − 29 —— U	51 − 25 —— P
71 − 23 —— O	93 − 18 —— S	53 − 29 —— E	81 − 19 —— A	37 − 28 —— T	63 − 17 —— L

Solve the Riddle!

Write the letter that goes with each number.

___ ___   ___ ___ ___
62   17   24   16   24

___ ___ ___ - ___ ___ ___ ___
3   24   9   17   24   75   75

Curious Creature

Read the story. Use details from the story to answer the questions below.

Zolak boarded his spaceship and blasted off from the planet Vartog. He was on a special mission to learn about Earthlings. His spaceship landed gently in a desert. Zolak walked around looking for Earthlings, but all he could see were rocks and sand. Then he looked down and saw a dark creature lying down right next to him. In fact, the creature's feet were touching Zolak's feet. Zolak was scared and tried to run away, but everywhere he went, the creature followed him. At noon, Zolak realized that the creature had shrunk to a very small size but was still right next to his feet. However, during the afternoon, the dark creature grew longer and longer! Then, the strangest thing happened. Night came and the dark creature completely disappeared.

1 What happens at the beginning of the story? _____

_____

2 Was the dark creature an Earthling?   ○ yes   ○ no

3 Who do you think the dark creature was? _____

4 What happens at the end of the story?

_____

_____

5 Do you think Zolak will give a true report
about Earthlings when he returns to Vartog? ○ yes   ○ no

Why or why not?

_____

_____

Compare Lengths: Centimeters

Use a ruler to measure the shapes below.
Record the length of each shape. Then find the difference.

Shape A

Shape B

Shape C

Shape D

1 Length of Shape A: _____ cm

Length of Shape B: _____ cm

Difference: _____ cm

2 Length of Shape C: _____ cm

Length of Shape D: _____ cm

Difference: _____ cm

Shape E

Shape F

Shape G

Shape H

3 Length of Shape E: _____ cm

Length of Shape F: _____ cm

Difference: _____ cm

4 Length of Shape G: _____ cm

Length of Shape H: _____ cm

Difference: _____ cm

Shape I

Shape J

5 Length of Shape I: _____ cm

Length of Shape J: _____ cm

Difference: _____ cm

Help Your Child Get Ready: Week 6

Here are some activities that you and your child might enjoy.

Mapping My World?

Invite your child to draw pictures and write labels to make maps of familiar places, such as his or her school, a local park, or a favorite friend's home.

Word Expert

Boost your child's vocabulary by playing "Word Expert." Tell him or her that for each word you say, he or she must give you a synonym and an antonym, as well as an example of the word. For instance, if you say *exciting*, a synonym might be *thrilling*, an antonym might be *boring*, and an example could be *riding a roller coaster*.

Nutrition Label Math

Show examples of food labels to your child, ideally those with more than one serving in a package. Talk about what the numbers on the label mean. Then ask your child to determine the nutrition totals for the entire item. For example, if there are 2 servings in a small can of vegetables, your child can double the nutrition label numbers to find the total calories, fat and carbohydrate content, and so on.

One-Minute Categories

Ask your child to name as many examples as possible of a category in one minute. For example, for *animals*, he or she might name *dog, cat, wolf, tiger*, and so on. Make the categories more challenging as his or her skill increases. You can also specify naming animals that start with a particular letter. For example, for the letter *d*, animals would include *dog, duck*, and *donkey*.

These are the skills your child will be working on this week.

Math
- solve problems involving money
- record data on a line plot
- measure and compare heights
- identify attributes of a shape

Reading
- identify key details
- use text features
- identify details about a character

Phonics & Vocabulary
- long-*u* sound
- short-vowel sounds with *-ing* and *-ed* endings
- differentiate *aw* and *all* sounds

Grammar & Writing
- punctuation: questions

Incentive Chart: Week 6

Week 6	Day 1	Day 2	Day 3	Day 4	Day 5
Put a sticker to show you completed each day's work.	☆ ☆	☆ ☆	☆ ☆	☆ ☆	☆ ☆

CONGRATULATIONS!

Wow! You did a great job this week!

This certificate is presented to:

_____

_____   _____
Date   Parent/Caregiver's Signature

The Cute Mule

The **long-*u*** sound can be spelled with the letters ***oo*** or ***u_e***.

Read and write each word on the lines below.
Watch for a word that has an unexpected spelling.
Then organize the words by the letters that make the long-*u* sound.

1 cute _____

2 mule _____

3 tube _____

4 room _____

5 moon _____

6 rule _____

7 spoon _____

8 food _____

9 tune _____

10 who _____

oo

_____

_____

_____

_____

u_e

_____

_____

_____

_____

unexpected spelling

_____

Change one letter in each word below to spell a word from the activity above.

1 cube _____ or _____

2 tube _____

3 spook _____

4 male _____

5 role _____

6 why _____

7 noon _____

8 zoom _____

9 fool _____

A Blowout Sale!

The store is having a sale! Circle the coins you would need to buy each item.
Circle the fewest number of coins possible.

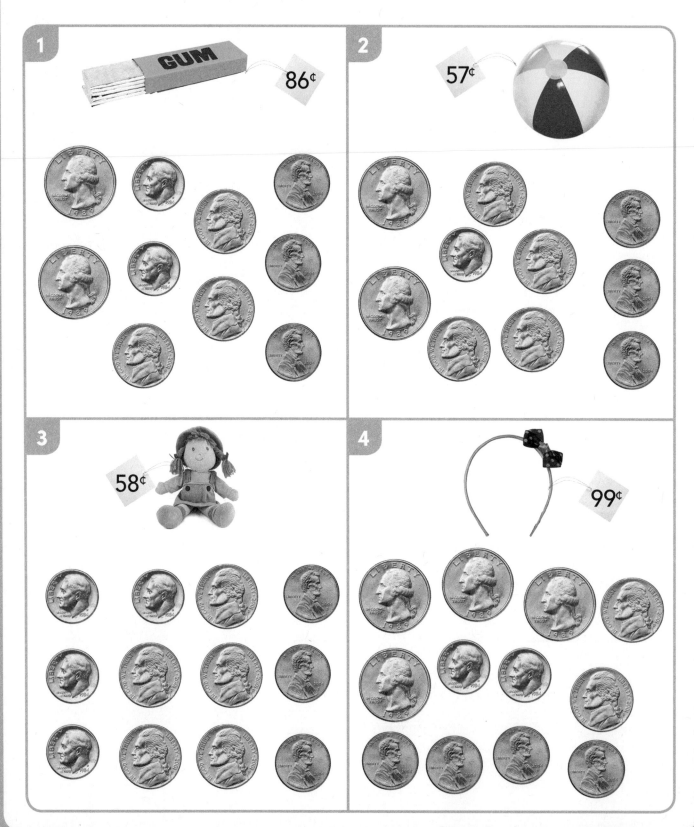

Hardworking Dogs

Read the article. Then answer the questions.

Many people serve in our armed forces. Some dogs do, too!

These dogs work hard, just like human soldiers. They are trained for a long time. They go where soldiers go, even when it's dangerous.

They help soldiers with different jobs. Dogs use their sense of smell to search for things. They help rescue people. They also protect soldiers.

This soldier is training the dog to jump high.

1 Underline the title.

2 What is this article about?

○ a dog show ○ dogs in the armed forces ○ soldiers

3 Which of these is NOT a way dogs help soldiers?

○ Dogs search for things.

○ Dogs dive deep underwater.

○ Dogs help rescue people.

4 Which would be another good title for this article?

○ Jumping Dogs ○ The Armed Forces ○ Dogs Help Soldiers

5 Read the caption. What is the dog doing?

○ being trained ○ searching ○ playing

Measure the Shape

Use a ruler to measure in centimeters each line segment below.
Then record the data on the line plot. The first one is done for you.

7cm

Ask Mother Goose

A sentence that asks a question ends with a **question mark** (?).
It often begins with one of these words:

Who	What	Where	When	Why	Will	Could

Rewrite the questions using capital letters and question marks.

1 where is the king's castle

_____

2 who helped Humpty Dumpty

_____

3 why did the cow jump over the moon

_____

4 will the frog become a prince

_____

5 could the three mice see

_____

Who Dropped the Ice Cream?

Each of these words has a short-vowel spelling with one final consonant. Before adding an ending such as **-ing** or **-ed**, double the final consonant.

Read and write each word on the lines below.
Underline the words with double consonants.
Then organize the words by their endings.

1 drop _____

2 dropped _____

3 beg _____

4 begged _____

5 skip _____

6 skipping _____

7 tap _____

8 tapping _____

9 run _____

10 running _____

no ending
_____
_____
_____
_____
_____

-ed ending
_____
_____

-ing ending
_____
_____
_____

Unscramble the letters to spell words from the activity above.

1 nunigrn _____

2 propedd _____

3 snigippk _____

4 dgebge _____

5 ipsk _____

6 patnpig _____

There Goes the Ball!

The letters **aw** make a sound in the word **law**. The letters **all** make the sound in the word **ball**. These are two different sounds.

Read and write each word on the lines below.
Then organize the words by either *aw* or *all*.

	aw	all
1 fall _____		
2 jaw _____	_____	_____
3 ball _____	_____	_____
4 hall _____	_____	_____
5 paw _____	_____	_____
6 saw _____	_____	_____
7 call _____	_____	_____
8 yawn _____		
9 draw _____		

Write a word from above that begins with the same letter as the picture.

 1 _____

 2 _____

 3 _____

 4 _____

 5 _____

 6 _____

 7 _____

 8 _____

 9 _____

Cool Penguins

This penguin family is part of a winter parade. They need to line up by height.
Give them a hand! Use a ruler to measure each penguin.
Label each penguin with its height in centimeters.

| **Paul** | **Peter** | **Patty** | **Petunia** |

Height: _____ cm   Height: _____ cm   Height: _____ cm   Height: _____ cm

Write the name of each penguin in order of height,
from the shortest to the tallest.

_____   _____   _____   _____
(shortest)   (tallest)

My Monster

Read the story.

I saw a scary monster that lived in a cave. It had shaggy fur and a long, striped tail. It had ugly, black teeth. Its three horns were shaped like arrows. Its nose was crooked. One of its feet was bigger than the other three. "Wake up! Time for breakfast," Mom said. Oh good! It was only a dream.

Read the directions below carefully. Follow the directions. Look for key words such as *circle, underline,* and *color*.

1 What did the monster's tail look like? Circle it.

2 What did the monster's teeth look like? Draw a box around them.

3 What did the monster's horns look like? Color them green.

4 What did the monster's nose look like? Underline it.

5 What did the monster's feet look like? Color them blue.

6 Which one of these is the correct picture of the monster? Draw a cave around it.

Polygons

All the shapes below are polygons.
Write the number of sides and angles of each shape.

1

sides _____

angles _____

2

sides _____

angles _____

3

sides _____

angles _____

4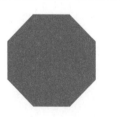

sides _____

angles _____

5

sides _____

angles _____

6

sides _____

angles _____

7

sides _____

angles _____

8

sides _____

angles _____

Help Your Child Get Ready: Week 7

Here are some activities that you and your child might enjoy.

Compliment Jar

Create a compliment jar by labeling a clear plastic jar with the word "Compliments." Invite everyone in your home to write a compliment for another family member on a slip of paper and place it in the jar. Once a week, invite your child to read the compliments aloud to the rest of the family. For a twist, turn it into a guessing game. Your child can read the compliment but leave out the name. Can anyone guess this person's identity? Your child can provide clues, if necessary.

"List-en" Up

Help your child develop good listening and memorization skills. Read a list of five items two times. Then ask your child to repeat the list back to you in order. Here is a list of the Great Lakes to get you started: Lake Erie, Lake Huron, Lake Michigan, Lake Ontario, Lake Superior.

Character Friends

Ask your child to talk about a character in one of the books he or she has been reading. You can prompt the discussion by asking questions such as: *Which characters would you want to be friends with in real life? What are some of the good qualities this character has? How are you and the character similar or different?*

Summer Games

Plan a mini "Summer Olympics" with your family. Play classic picnic games such as a water-balloon toss or a three-legged race, or make up fun games of your own. Take turns trying them!

These are the skills your child will be working on this week.

Math

- partition rectangles
- subtract 2 digits with and without regrouping
- add and subtract 100
- read a bar graph
- solve problems involving money

Reading

- fluency
- identify rhythm in a poem

Phonics & Vocabulary

- multiple-meaning words
- long-*u* sound
- compound words

Grammar & Writing

- use adjectives

Incentive Chart: Week 7

Week 7	Day 1	Day 2	Day 3	Day 4	Day 5
Put a sticker to show you completed each day's work.	☆ ☆	☆ ☆	☆ ☆	☆ ☆	☆ ☆

CONGRATULATIONS!

Wow! You did a great job this week!

This certificate is presented to:

_____

_____   _____
Date   Parent/Caregiver's Signature

Multiple-Meaning Words

Many words have more than one meaning. These words are called **multiple-meaning words.** The chart below shows some multiple-meaning words.

bat	bat	bowl	bowl	fly	fly
left	left	seal	seal	sink	sink

Next to each picture, write the number of the sentence that matches best.

1 Jeremy will **bat** next.

2 Small boats can **sink** in heavy storms.

3 Paula uses the green **bowl** for her cereal.

4 I forgot my keys and **left** them at home.

5 A **fly** landed on our picnic basket.

6 I saw a **bat** flying around in the attic.

7 Turn **left** at the corner.

8 Some birds **fly** to warmer places in winter.

9 Wash your hands in the **sink** before dinner.

10 I saw a young **seal** at the beach.

11 My brother likes to **bowl**.

12 Be sure to **seal** the envelope before mailing it.

____   ____

____   ____

____   ____

____   ____

____

____  ____

Break It Up!

Draw lines to break the shapes into small squares of equal size.
Write the total number of small squares on the line below each shape.
The first one is done for you.

1

5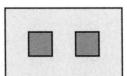

8 squares
_____

_____

2

6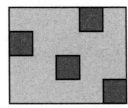

_____

_____

3

7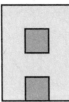

_____

_____

4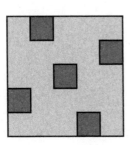

8

_____

_____

A True Blue Friend

When the **long-u** sound is found at the end of a word, it can be spelled with the letters **ew** or **ue**.

Read and write each word on the lines below.
Watch for a word that has an unexpected spelling.
Then organize the words by the letters that make the long-*u* sound.

1 flew _____

2 new _____

3 true _____

4 blue _____

5 grew _____

6 few _____

7 glue _____

8 drew _____

9 threw _____

10 two _____

ew
_____
_____
_____
_____
_____
_____

ue
_____
_____
_____

unexpected spelling
_____

Change the first and last letters of each word to spell a word from the activity above.

1 grub _____

2 owl _____

3 sled _____

4 let _____ and _____

5 club _____ and _____

Why is the octopus crossing the road?

Subtract.
Solve the riddle using your answers below.

86 − 32 _____ E	61 − 46 _____ F	63 − 29 _____ T	76 − 35 _____ P	94 − 56 _____ K	89 − 67 _____ O
96 − 69 _____ G	89 − 23 _____ N	64 − 14 _____ R	42 − 25 _____ S	86 − 11 _____ I	70 − 27 _____ A

Solve the Riddle!

Write the letter that goes with each number.

___ ___ ___ ___ ___ ___ ___ ___ ___
34 22   27 54 34   43   41 54 66

___ ___ ___ ___ ___ ___ ___ ___ ___
15 22 50   75 34 17   75 66 38

Mystery Boxes

Describing words help you imagine how something looks, feels, smells, sounds, or tastes.

Read the describing words to guess the mystery object.
Use the words in the Word Bank.

Word Bank

ball	bat	blanket	cracker

**soft
puffy
warm**

I am a _____

**hard
wood
long**

I am a _____

**square
dry
crisp**

I am a _____

**round
bouncy
red**

I am a _____

Add and Subtract

Above each number, write the number that is 100 more.
Below each number, write the number that is 100 less.
The first one is done for you.

319		
1 219	**5** 573	**9** 452
119		

2 209	**6** 499	**10** 323

3 456	**7** 700	**11** 554

4 233	**8** 608	**12** 817

Adding Words

A **compound noun** is made up of two smaller words put together.

Can you figure out what these compound nouns are?
Read the clues. Then write the compound noun.

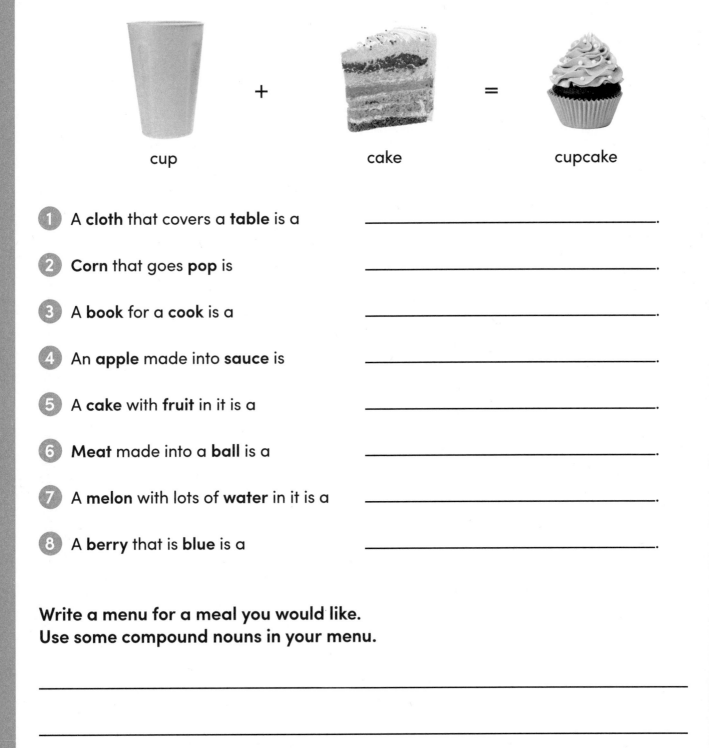

cup   +   cake   =   cupcake

1 A **cloth** that covers a **table** is a _____.

2 **Corn** that goes **pop** is _____.

3 A **book** for a **cook** is a _____.

4 An **apple** made into **sauce** is _____.

5 A **cake** with **fruit** in it is a _____.

6 **Meat** made into a **ball** is a _____.

7 A **melon** with lots of **water** in it is a _____.

8 A **berry** that is **blue** is a _____.

Write a menu for a meal you would like.
Use some compound nouns in your menu.

_____

_____

_____

Bamboo Graph

Bamboo is a super-plant. It can grow much taller than people. It can be as big as a tree. But bamboo is actually a kind of grass. The graph below shows how much a new bamboo plant grew over time. Use the graph to answer the questions.

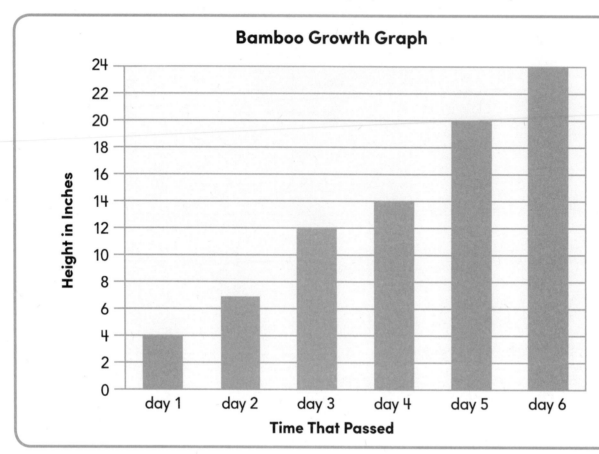

Bamboo Growth Graph

1 How tall was the bamboo on the fifth day?

○ 4 inches   ○ 14 inches   ○ 20 inches

2 How old was the bamboo when it was 14 inches tall?

○ 1 day old   ○ 4 days old   ○ 5 days old

3 How much did the bamboo grow between the fourth and the fifth day?

○ 1 inch   ○ 3 inches   ○ 6 inches

4 A foot is 12 inches. How many days old was the bamboo when it was 1 foot tall?

○ 2 days old   ○ 3 days old   ○ 4 days old

5 How many feet tall was the bamboo on the sixth day? _____

Did You Feed My Cow?

Read the poem aloud. Then underline the words that create rhythm in the poem.

Did you feed my cow.

Yes, Ma'am!

Will you tell me how?

Yes, Ma'am!

Oh, what did you give her?

Corn and hay.

Oh, what did you give her?

Corn and hay.

Did you milk her good?

Yes, Ma'am!

Did you do like you should?

Yes, Ma'am!

Oh, how did you milk her?

Swish! Swish! Swish!

Oh, how did you milk her?

Swish! Swish! Swish!

Exact Change, Please

Read each amount on the left. Write the exact number of coins needed to exactly total the amount. There are many combinations you might make, but you must pick the fewest coins possible. The first one is done for you.

Example: You could make 33¢ with 3 dimes and 3 pennies, but this would take 6 coins. Using a quarter, a nickel, and 3 pennies uses just 5 coins.

	Quarter 25¢	Dime 10¢	Nickel 5¢	Penny 1¢
33¢	1		1	3
85¢				
24¢				
65¢				
$1.16				
58¢				
$2.05				
12¢				
$3.25				
73¢				

How many nickels do you need to make $2? _____

Help Your Child Get Ready: Week 8

Here are some activities that you and your child might enjoy.

Spinning Stories

Cut out ten pictures from a magazine. Put them in a bag. Invite your child to take them out two or three at a time and use the pictures to tell a story.

Twenty Questions

This favorite game can be used to build thinking skills. First choose a category, such as *animals*. Then think of one animal. Tell your child that he or she can ask only "yes" or "no" questions to determine the animal you are thinking of. Once he or she gets the hang of it, take turns thinking of an animal while the other asks questions.

Going Acrostic

Provide opportunities for your child to create "acrostic" poems. To begin an acrostic poem, first write any word vertically (you may wish to start with your child's name). Then your child uses each letter of the word as the first letter in another word—one that relates to the original word—and writes that word horizontally.

Food Fractions

Fractions are fun to practice using foods like pizza or various fruits. With your child, define the whole item. Then divide it in half, quarters, eighths, or more. What is the smallest piece you can make?

These are the skills your child will be working on this week.

Math

- compare 3-digit numbers
- write numbers in standard form
- tell time: 5-, 10-, and 20-minute increments
- add 3 digits without regrouping
- add 3 digits with regrouping

Reading

- use text features
- identify author's purpose

Phonics & Vocabulary

- compound words
- short-*oo* sound

Grammar & Writing

- punctuation: statements and questions
- contractions

Incentive Chart: Week 8

Week 8	Day 1	Day 2	Day 3	Day 4	Day 5
Put a sticker to show you completed each day's work.	☆ ☆	☆ ☆	☆ ☆	☆ ☆	☆ ☆

CONGRATULATIONS!

Wow! You did a great job this week!

This certificate is presented to:

_____

_____   _____
Date   Parent/Caregiver's Signature

Sunny Sentences

Every sentence begins with a **capital letter**.
A **telling sentence** ends with a **period (.)**.
An **asking sentence** ends with a **question mark (?)**.

Rewrite each sentence correctly.

1 the sun is the closest star to Earth

_____

2 the sun is not the brightest star

_____

3 what is the temperature of the sun

_____

4 the sun is a ball of hot gas

_____

5 how large is the sun

_____

6 it takes about 8 minutes for the sun's light to reach Earth

_____

_____

Greater, Less, or Equal?

Compare the numbers. Use the symbols <, >, or =.

1. 300 ◯ 261

2. 205 ◯ 612

3. 685 ◯ 685

4. 744 ◯ 477

5. 918 ◯ 991

6. 154 ◯ 211

7. 398 ◯ 396

8. 499 ◯ 137

9. 932 ◯ 941

10. 357 ◯ 357

11. 423 ◯ 500

12. 599 ◯ 603

13. 221 ◯ 221

14. 824 ◯ 823

15. 547 ◯ 544

16. 871 ◯ 817

17. 925 ◯ 986

18. 613 ◯ 761

Side by Side

A **compound word** is made up of two smaller words put together.

Complete the crossword puzzle with the missing part of each compound word. Use the Word Bank to help you.

Word Bank

ball	bath	brush	bed	cake	down	farm	finger
flower	ground	hive	knob	lid	plane	shelf	walk

Across

3. cup_____

5. _____house

6. sun_____

9. _____print

10. door_____

11. tooth_____

14. air_____

15. eye_____

Down

1. book_____

2. _____tub

4. under_____

7. side_____

8. _____time

9. sun_____

12. bee_____

13. foot_____

Standard Numbers

Write each number in standard form.

1 $80 + 4 =$ _____

2 $30 + 9 =$ _____

3 $70 + 8 =$ _____

$500 + 50 + 7 =$
557

4 $10 + 2 =$ _____

5 $50 + 7 =$ _____

6 $40 + 9 =$ _____

7 $300 + 80 + 60 =$ _____

8 $400 + 70 + 5 =$ _____

9 $600 + 40 + 3 =$ _____

10 $100 + 30 + 2 =$ _____

11 $900 + 30 + 8 =$ _____

12 $200 + 60 + 4 =$ _____

A Good Book

The letters **u, oo,** and **ou** can all sound like **oo** in **good**.

Read and write each word on the lines below.
Then organize the words by the letters that make the short-*oo* sound.

1 good _____

2 book _____

3 put _____

4 could _____

5 look _____

6 pull _____

7 would _____

8 push _____

9 foot _____

10 should _____

u

_____

_____

_____

ou

_____

_____

_____

oo

_____

_____

_____

_____

Circle the word that is spelled correctly.

1 shood   should

2 foot   fout

3 pul   pull

4 louk   look

5 cood   could

6 book   booke

7 put   poot

8 gude   good

What does Pinocchio feed his wooden dog?

Read the clocks. Write the times. Solve the riddle using your answers below.

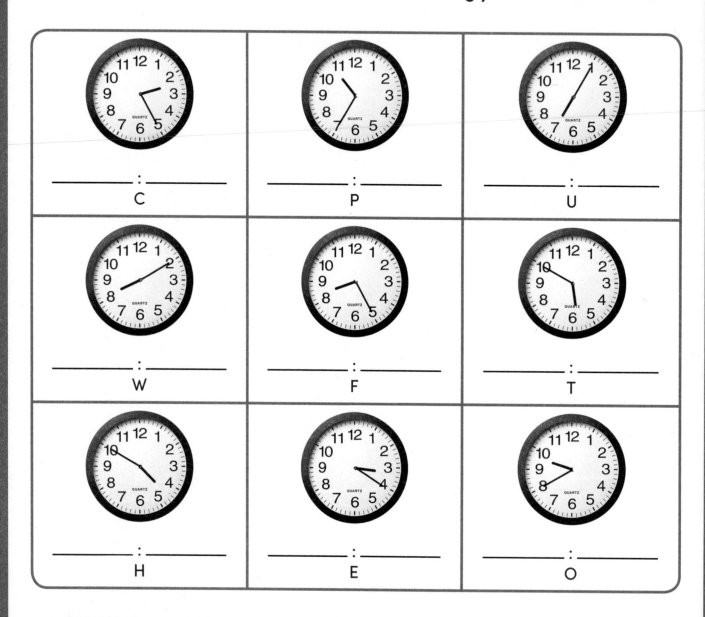

_____ : _____
C

_____ : _____
P

_____ : _____
U

_____ : _____
W

_____ : _____
F

_____ : _____
T

_____ : _____
H

_____ : _____
E

_____ : _____
O

Solve the Riddle!

Write the letter that goes with each time.

____ ____ ____ ____ ____ ____   ____ ____ ____ ____
10:35   7:05   10:35 10:35   3:20   5:50   2:25   4:50   9:40   8:10

Contraction Action

A **contraction** is a fast way to join words together.
One or more letters in the second word are left out and replaced by an apostrophe.

Example: *there is* becomes *there's*

Write the missing words or contractions.
The first one is done for you.

1 ____was____ + not = wasn't

2 I + am = _____

3 is + _____ = isn't

4 here + is = _____

5 you + _____ = you're

6 _____ + not = doesn't

7 they + have = _____

8 we + will = _____

9 should + _____ = should've

10 let + us = _____

11 who + is = _____

12 you + would = _____

13 who + _____ = who've

14 we + are = _____

What happens once in every minute, twice in every moment, but not once in a hundred years?

Add. Solve the riddle using your answers below.

121 + 124 ___ E	322 + 145 ___ N	420 + 166 ___ R	104 + 264 ___ T	272 + 302 ___ A	131 + 251 ___ O
211 + 131 ___ L	140 + 413 ___ B	210 + 235 ___ F	126 + 131 ___ D	310 + 119 ___ H	123 + 141 ___ M

Solve the Riddle!

Write the letter that goes with each number.

___ ___ ___
368 429 245

___ ___ ___ ___ ___ ___   ___
342 245 368 368 245 586   264

Splash Into Safety

Read the article. Then answer the questions below.

Whether it's catching waves at the beach or doing a cannonball in the pool, summer is a great time for a swim! Before you take a dip, check out these water safety tips.

Play nicely and calmly in the water. Don't push people, even if it's just for fun.

Around the pool, walk—don't run. That will help keep you from falling.

And always swim with a buddy. Make sure there's a lifeguard or an adult nearby, too. It's more fun to swim with company, and you'll stay safe all summer long!

1 Which of these is NOT a way to stay safe?

○ Play calmly. ○ Swim alone. ○ Walk, don't run.

2 What would be another good title for the article?

○ Lifeguard Training ○ Wear Sunscreen! ○ Water-Safety Tips

3 Which of these would make the best caption for the photo above?

○ Lifeguards help keep us safe in the water.
○ Make sure to wear bug spray when you hike.
○ Many surfers wear wet suits.

4 What is the author trying to do in this article?

○ give helpful tips about water safety
○ tell an exciting story about swimming
○ convince you to swim at a pool

Twin Test

These twins just took a math test. All the twins passed the test, but only one set of twins got all the answers right. To find out which, solve the addition problems under each child. The twins that got all the answers right have problems with the same answer. Circle the twins.

$$277 \\ + 545$$

$$145 \\ + 189$$

$$315 \\ + 248$$

$$229 \\ + 418$$

$$547 \\ + 129$$

$$624 \\ + 127$$

$$108 \\ + 107$$

$$247 \\ + 558$$

$$368 \\ + 268$$

$$379 \\ + 336$$

$$417 \\ + 109$$

$$153 \\ + 494$$

Help Your Child Get Ready: Week 9

Here are some activities that you and your child might enjoy.

Math in a Menu

When you and your child are looking at a menu, take the opportunity to practice math concepts. Ask questions such as: *Which food item costs the most? How much is it? Which item costs the least? If you bought the most expensive and the least expensive items, how much would you spend altogether?*

Summer Fun With A–Z

Ask your child to think about what he or she loves about summer. Then challenge him or her to write about these things in sentences that use all 26 letters of the alphabet. Encourage your child to circle each letter the first time it is used.

Double Meanings

Reinforce the concept of homophones with your child by challenging him or her to find two or more meanings for each of these words: *bob, fair, lock, pitcher.* Come up with more homophones to challenge your child further.

How Puzzling!

Invite your child to create a jigsaw puzzle. Provide a large sheet of paper, crayons or colored markers, and scissors. First your child can draw a picture. Then he or she can cut it up into smaller pieces and mix them up. See if you or another family member can put it back together!

These are the skills your child will be working on this week.

Math

- solve problems involving money
- subtract 3 digits without regrouping
- linear measurements
- add three 2-digit numbers
- compare lengths

Reading

- compare and contrast
- use context clues

Phonics & Vocabulary

- prefix *un–*
- vowel digraphs

Incentive Chart: Week 9

Week 9	Day 1	Day 2	Day 3	Day 4	Day 5
Put a sticker to show you completed each day's work.	☆ ☆	☆ ☆	☆ ☆	☆ ☆	☆ ☆

CONGRATULATIONS!

Wow! You did a great job this week!

This certificate is presented to:

_____

_____   _____
Date   Parent/Caregiver's Signature

How Unusual!

The prefix **un-** means either "not" or "do the opposite of" the base of the word.

Circle each base word in the puzzle. The words go →, ↓, ↗, and ↘.
The first one is done for you.

Word Bank

~~unpack~~	untie	unload	unlock	unwind	undo
unknown	unfold	unable	unfair	unusual	unwise

```
R   A   I   L   I   M   A   F   X
N   E   E   O   F   F   O   L   D
I   W   E   A   W   A   X   L   E
A   I   X   D   L   I   I   O   T
T   S   K   N   O   W   N   R   N
R   E   V   O   C   Z   R   D   I
E   P   A   C   K   X   E   A   A
C   A   B   L   E   S   Y   Z   P
D   N   I   K   U   S   U   A   L
```

Write a word from the Word Bank to complete each sentence.

1 It is _____ for James to be late for school.

2 It took me ten minutes to _____ the knot.

3 You need a key to _____ the trunk.

4 We grew more interested as the story began to _____.

5 It is _____ to wait until the last minute to do your homework.

6 Bill thought the umpire's call was _____.

Sandwich Shop

How much did each friend spend at the diner? Add to find out.

Menu

hot dog	$2.53	fruit salad	$2.90
blt	$2.49	veggies & dip	$2.84
turkey sub	$3.86	chips	$0.75
hamburger	$3.72	fries	$1.05
juice	$1.04	cupcake	$1.50
milk	$0.95	brownie	$1.95
shake	$2.17	cookies	$0.86

Sally

blt

chips

milk

brownie   +

_____

Kamal

hamburger

fries

shake   +

_____

Min

turkey sub

veggies & dip

juice

cupcake   +

_____

Roberto

hot dog

fruit salad

brownie

juice   +

_____

Michelle

turkey sub

chips

shake   +

_____

Chet

blt

cookies

milk   +

_____

Vowel Digraph Outlaws

Vowel digraphs are two vowels, such as **ea,** that make one sound.
Usually the first vowel is long, and the second one is silent. For example:

ea words:	**tēam**	**lēaf**	*ey* words:	**monkēy**	**donkēy**
ie words:	**piė**	**tiėd**	*ei* words:	**cēiling**	**protēin**

But some words do not follow the rules. For example:

ea words:	**bread**	**early**	*ey* words:	**obey**	**prey**
ie words:	**piece**	**shield**	*ei* words:	**height**	**eight**

The underlined words in the sentences below have vowel digraphs that
do not follow the rules. What is the correct pronunciation of each word?
Next to each, write the letter of the picture that best illustrates the sentence.

1 This <u>steak</u> tastes <u>great</u>!

2 <u>Spread</u> some jam on the <u>bread</u>.

3 Trey said, "<u>Hey</u>, <u>they</u> won!"

4 The police <u>chief</u> saw a <u>thief</u> stealing <u>pennies</u>.

5 <u>Eight</u> <u>neighbors</u> rode in a <u>sleigh</u>.

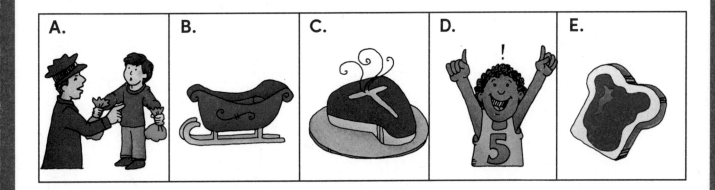

A.   B.   C.   D.   E.

Why is the lion crossing the road?

Subtract.
Solve the riddle using your answers below.

424 − 121	299 − 107	576 − 130	698 − 541	379 − 101	867 − 125
_____	_____	_____	_____	_____	_____
E	P	R	T	A	L
445 − 234	947 − 113	878 − 242	536 − 131	787 − 207	679 − 310
_____	_____	_____	_____	_____	_____
N	G	O	D	I	H

Solve the Riddle!

Write the letter that goes with each number.

___ ___   ___ ___ ___   ___ ___   ___ ___ ___
157 636   834 303 157   157 636   157 369 303

___ ___ ___ ___ ___   ___ ___ ___ ___ ___
636 157 369 303 446   192 446 580 405 303

Zoo Reports

Compare means to look for things that are the same.
Contrast means to look for things that are different

The second-grade class went to the zoo on a field trip. The next day, the teacher asked the children to write a report about what they learned. Read the two reports below.

Ryan

<u>What I Learned at the Zoo</u>

I learned about the giant tortoise. They eat grasses, plants, and cacti. They can weigh up to 450 pounds. Some tortoises live to be over 100 years old! That's older than my grandpa!

The slowest-moving mammal is the three-toed sloth. It hangs from trees and eats fruit. Some sloths sleep more than 20 hours a day. What a lazy animal!

I thought the albino alligator was really cool. It wasn't green. It was completely white all over. It was born that way.

Jessica

<u>What I Learned at the Zoo</u>

The tallest animal on earth is the giraffe. It eats leaves from the tops of the trees. Giraffes come from Africa.

I learned about an albino alligator. It was white instead of green. The guide told us that it was born without the coloring of other alligators.

I saw an owl sleeping in a tree. Owls sleep in the daytime and hunt at night. When they sleep, they don't fall out of the tree because they have sharp claws that lock onto the branch.

Ryan and Jessica each wrote about three animals. Write the names of the animals they wrote about in the correct circles. In the center, where both circles overlap, write the name of the animal that they both wrote about.

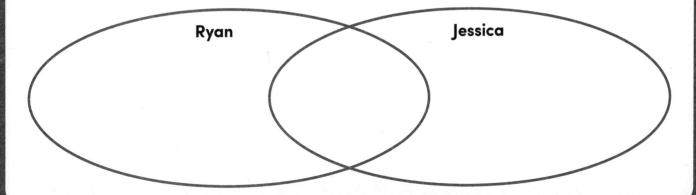

Measurement Match-Ups

Measurements of Length

12 inches = 1 foot   36 inches = 1 yard   3 feet = 1 yard

Next to each measurement in the left column, write the letter of the measurement in the right column that is equal in length.

1 24 inches _____   **a.** 6 inches

2 6 feet _____   **b.** 4 yards

3 18 inches _____   **c.** 9 feet

4 36 inches _____   **d.** 2 feet

5 12 feet _____   **e.** 4 feet

6 60 inches _____   **f.** $\frac{1}{3}$ foot

7 4 inches _____   **g.** $1\frac{1}{2}$ feet

8 3 yards _____   **h.** 2 yards

9 48 inches _____   **i.** 5 feet

10 $\frac{1}{2}$ foot _____   **j.** 1 yard

A Silly Riddle

How many feet are in a yard?

Answer: That depends on how many people are standing in it.

It Means . . .

Read each sentence.
Use the words in the sentence to figure out the meaning of the underlined word.
Circle the word or phrase that has a similar meaning to the underlined word.

1 This large vase will be <u>ideal</u> for that huge bunch of flowers.

    ready   perfect   ugly

2 If you do me this favor, I will be <u>eternally</u> thankful.

    quickly   sadly   forever

3 The strong motor <u>propelled</u> the boat quickly through the water.

    sunk   pushed   swam

4 Those two do not get along. They <u>quarrel</u> all the time.

    laugh   work   argue

5 I had not eaten all day and by night time I was <u>ravenous</u>.

    starving   tired   bored

6 While sitting in my chair, I <u>elevated</u> my feet onto the desk.

    lifted   washed   threw

7 These tickets are not <u>valid</u> anymore.
You were supposed to have used them yesterday.

    torn   cheap   good

8 The <u>artificial</u> flowers were made of plastic.

    fake   real   red

Carnival Fun

Solve the problems below. Find your answers hidden in the carnival scene.
Circle each. Can you find all twelve answers?

15	27	34	15	16	12
33	23	23	25	14	31
+ 27	+ 12	+ 34	+ 10	+ 14	+ 17

28	43	10	29	37	51
22	27	17	13	31	23
+ 45	+ 27	+ 18	+ 16	+ 17	+ 27

Working Animals

Many animals work to help people. Some animals help rescue people. Others help people with special needs.

Read the articles below. Then answer the questions.

Avalanche Dog	Service Horse

In an avalanche, people can get trapped under the snow. Other people can't hear them call for help. Avalanche dogs sniff for trapped people. The dogs bark and dig if they find someone.	This is a miniature horse. It is very small. Service horses help in many ways. They pick things up for people with their mouths. People who need help walking can hold on to them. This horse wears shoes so it doesn't slip.

1 Which animal wears shoes?

   ○ avalanche dog   ○ service horse   ○ Chief

2 How do avalanche dogs help people?

   ○ sniff for trapped people   ○ pick up things with their mouths   ○ carry

3 What can service horses help people do?

   ○ sniff for trapped people   ○ turn on lights   ○ walk

4 What is something a service horse and an avalanche dog both do?

   ○ bark if someone needs help

   ○ wear shoes

   ○ help people

Compare Lengths

Use a ruler to measure the shapes below.
Record the length of each shape. Then find the difference.

| Shape A |
| Shape B |

| Shape C |
| Shape D |

1 Length of Shape A: _____ cm

Length of Shape B: _____ cm

Difference: _____ cm

2 Length of Shape C: _____ cm

Length of Shape D: _____ cm

Difference: _____ cm

| Shape E |
| Shape F |

| Shape G |
| Shape H |

3 Length of Shape E: _____ cm

Length of Shape F: _____ cm

Difference: _____ cm

4 Length of Shape G: _____ cm

Length of Shape H: _____ cm

Difference: _____ cm

| Shape I |
| Shape J |

5 Length of Shape I: _____ cm

Length of Shape J: _____ cm

Difference: _____ cm

Help Your Child Get Ready: Week 10

Here are some activities that you and your child might enjoy.

Snappy Summaries

Writing a summary is often hard for children. To help your child sharpen this important skill, have him or her create one-sentence summaries of favorite books, movies, or television shows. Ask your child to think about this question: *Who did what, when, and why?*

Comic Mix-Up

Build up your child's sequencing skills. Cut a comic strip into sections. Ask your child to put the strip in the correct order and to explain his or her thinking.

Wonderful Window

Invite your child to look out a window. Then ask: *What do you see that begins with the letter W?* See if your child can name five things. You can try this with other letters as well.

Travel Brochure

Together with your child, create a "travel brochure" for someplace you have been over the summer. For example, the place could be as local as a neighborhood swimming pool or park, or a distant place that was part of a vacation. Write about the place and remember to include pictures, either illustrations found in magazines, or if possible, real photographs.

These are the skills your child will be working on this week.

Math

- add and subtract 3 digits with and without regrouping

- use a bar graph

- solve word problems

- add three 2-digit numbers

Reading

- sequence

- identify author's purpose

- identify key details

Phonics & Vocabulary

- prefixes: *re-, dis-, in-, im-, un-*

- synonyms

- vowel digraphs

Incentive Chart: Week 10

Week 10	Day 1	Day 2	Day 3	Day 4	Day 5
Put a sticker to show you completed each day's work.	☆ ☆	☆ ☆	☆ ☆	☆ ☆	☆ ☆

CONGRATULATIONS!

Wow! You did a great job this week!

This certificate is presented to:

_____

_____   _____
Date   Parent/Caregiver's Signature

Let's Do the Opposite

When the prefix *re-* is put at the beginning of the word *heat*, the word's new meaning is "to heat again." Here are some prefixes that mean "not" or "the opposite of."

dis-	in-	im-	un-

Read each description below. Write a new word on the lines that means the same. The new word should use the prefix *dis-, in-, im-* or *un-*.

1 not helpful _____ _____ _____ _____ _____ _____ _____
　　　　　　　　　9　　　　　　　　　　　　　　11

2 not patient _____ _____ _____ _____ _____ _____ _____
　　　　　　　　　　　　　　　　4　　　　　2

3 not tied _____ _____ _____ _____ _____
　　　　　　　　　　10

4 not correct _____ _____ _____ _____ _____ _____
　　　　　　　　　　　　　7　　　12

5 not honest _____ _____ _____ _____ _____ _____
　　　　　　　3　　　　　1　　　　14

6 not possible _____ _____ _____ _____ _____ _____ _____ _____
　　　　　　　　　　　8

7 not agree _____ _____ _____ _____ _____
　　　　　　　　5　　　13

8 not fair _____ _____ _____ _____ _____
　　　　　　　　6

To find the answer to the question below, write the letter that goes with each number.

Where are a cricket's ears?

_____ _____ _____ _____ _____ _____ _____ _____ _____ _____ _____ _____ _____ _____
　1　　2　　　3　　4　　5　　　6　　7　　8　　9　　10　　　11　　12　　13　　14

What game do little monsters like to play?

Subtract.
Solve the riddle using your answers below.

748 − 437 ——— F	574 − 419 ——— E	133 + 129 ——— S	317 + 487 ——— T	738 − 218 ——— I	629 + 298 ——— N
937 − 248 ——— A	323 + 413 ——— H	754 − 276 ——— K	585 + 279 ——— D	354 − 257 ——— R	141 + 102 ——— M

Solve the Riddle!

Write the letter that goes with each number.

___ ___ ___ ___   ___ ___ ___
736 520 864 155   689 927 864

___ ___ ___ ___ ___ ___
262 736 97 520 155 478

The Outdoors

> **Synonyms** are words that mean nearly the same thing.

Read each sentence.
Circle the word that means almost the same as the underlined word.

1 Tom was outside for <u>just</u> five minutes.

after   only   over

2 Please <u>save</u> this seat for me.

bring   buy   keep

3 The three bears lived in the <u>woods</u>.

forest   house   tent

4 Pam went to bed because she was <u>sleepy</u>.

quiet   tired   awake

5 First the cat <u>sniffed</u> the food, then she ate it.

smelled   pulled   pushed

6 Mary <u>tore</u> her best dress.

mended   ripped   broke

7 The teacher <u>spoke</u> in a soft voice.

cheered   talked   screamed

8 I am <u>glad</u> that the flower has bloomed.

angry   asking   happy

Seashells by the Seashore

Sally sees seashells by the seashore and collects them each summer. To learn how many seashells she has collected over the years, study the bar graph below.

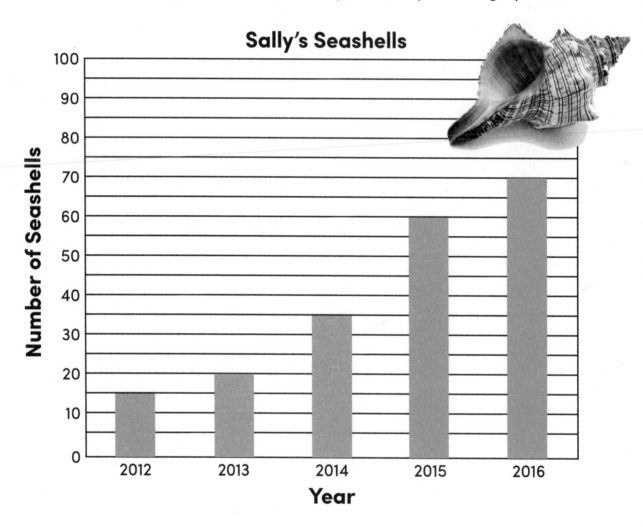

Use the information in the bar graph to answer the questions.

1 How many shells did Sally collect in 2012? _____

2 How many shells did Sally collect in 2015? _____

3 How many more shells did Sally collect in 2016 than in 2012? _____

4 In which years did Sally collect an odd number of shells? _____

5 All together, how many shells did Sally collect? _____

Hunter

Read each sentence below.

Then Sarah brought Hunter home.

As Sarah walked down the street, a big dog ran towards her.

Then Sarah realized that she knew the dog.

Sarah hugged Hunter when he got to her.

Her face turned white with fear.

Its name was Hunter.

The sentences above tell a story but they are out of order. Rewrite the sentences in the correct order. Then read the story.

_____

_____

_____

_____

_____

_____

Animal Facts

Add or subtract.

T 247 + 253	O 463 + 440	L 139 + 146	P 639 + 207	A 391 + 144	W 459 + 492	I 198 + 672
P 842 − 314	L 504 + 475	I 500 − 293	R 457 + 364	I 903 − 339	O 107 + 147	A 924 − 108
N 700 − 427	N 983 − 174	R 703 − 186	H 258 + 553	A 357 + 537		

Move across each row. Write the letter from each box with the correct number of hundreds in the order in which they appear.

2 hundreds	I am a cat that likes to sleep 20 hours a day.	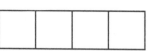

5 hundreds	I have four toes on my front feet and three toes on my back feet.	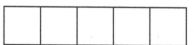

8 hundreds	I am a fish with razor-sharp teeth.	

9 hundreds	I can see well at night but cannot move my eyes.	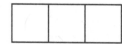

More Rule Breakers

In a **vowel digraph**, usually the first vowel is long and the second one is silent. However, in some words, both vowel sounds are heard. For example, you hear not one but two vowel sounds in *diet* and *neon*.

Read the words in the list below. Do you hear two vowel sounds? Draw a line from each word to the picture that matches it.

quiet

Brian

ruined

pliers

duet

fuel

science

lion

125

Food Frenzy!

Solve each word problem on the left and right. Draw a line to match each answer on the left with one on the right that is the same. (NOTE: Only the numbers have to match.)

Left

1 After a great win, Jeanette's soccer team went out to eat. There were nine people and they ordered 27 slices of pizza. If everyone had the same number of slices, how many did they each eat?

_____

2 Five teammates equally shared 30 chicken nuggets. How many did they each eat?

_____

3 Each of the eight people drank eight ounces of water. How many ounces did they drink in all?

_____

4 The waiter brought a plate with 20 pieces of vegetables to the table. The team ate 13 of them. How many were left?

_____

Right

A. Four teammates ordered ice cream for dessert. If they shared 12 scoops equally, how many scoops did each player eat?

_____

B. Jeanette had a plate with 38 pieces of fruit for desert. She ate 31 pieces and gave the rest to Mark. How many did Mark get?

_____

C. Each of the two coaches paid $32 for the meal. How much was the total cost?

_____

D. At first, the coaches gave $70 to pay for the meal. How much change did they get back? (Hint: Your answer to C, above, will help you solve the problem.)

_____

At Home in the Cold

Read the story.
Then, answer the questions below.

For most of the year, elephant seals swim in the icy ocean and hunt for fish and squid. The ocean water is very cold, but elephant seals don't freeze. A thick layer of fat called blubber keeps them warm.

The seals are great swimmers. Their big flippers and rocket-shaped bodies help them zoom through water. They can dive deeper than 7,000 feet under the water and hold their breath for two hours!

In summer, elephant seals come on land to shed their skin and fur. This helps keep them healthy and clean.

In spring, the females have babies. When the babies are about two-and-a-half months old, they leave the land and go into the ocean. They have grown big and strong enough to swim and hunt on their own!

1 What is this author describing in this article?

_____

2 Write a sentence from the article that tells why elephant seals don't freeze in the ocean water.

_____

_____

3 Write a sentence from the article that tells why elephant seals are great swimmers.

_____

_____

Green Light for Addition

Without numbers on their cars, the racers won't get very far.
Add up the numbers on each stoplight.
Write your answer on the blank below each stoplight.

1 Race car
number = _____

4 Race car
number = _____

7 Race car
number = _____

2 Race car
number = _____

5 Race car
number = _____

8 Race car
number = _____

9 Race car
number = _____

3 Race car
number = _____

6 Race car
number = _____

9 Race car
number = _____

Who won the race? Here are a few hints . . .

The winning car's number has two digits.

Both numbers are the same.

Which car won? _____

Answer Key

Week 1

A Group of Nouns

Nouns name people, places, and things. Special nouns name groups. These nouns are called collective nouns. A **collective noun** names a group of animals, people, or things.

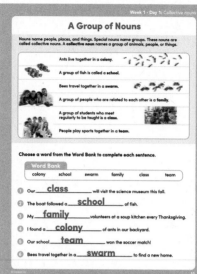

Ants live together in a colony.	
A group of fish is called a school.	
Bees travel together in a swarm.	
A group of people who are related to each other is a family.	
A group of students who meet regularly to be taught is a class.	
People play sports together in a team.	

Choose a word from the Word Bank to complete each sentence.

Word Bank

colony   school   swarm   family   class   team

1. Our **class** will visit the science museum this fall.
2. The boat followed a **school** of fish.
3. My **family** volunteers at a soup kitchen every Thanksgiving.
4. I found a **colony** of ants in our backyard.
5. Our school **team** won the soccer match!
6. Bees travel together in a **swarm** to find a new home.

11

Possessive Nouns

A **possessive noun** shows ownership. Add **'s** to make a singular noun show ownership. Add an **apostrophe (')** after the **s** of a plural noun to show ownership.

Underline the possessive noun in each sentence. Write S on the line if the possessive noun is singular. Write P if the possessive noun is plural.

1. Anna's family took a walk in the woods. — **S**
2. They saw two birds' nests high up in a tree. — **P**
3. A yellow butterfly landed on Brad's backpack. — **S**
4. Anna liked the pattern of the butterfly's wings. — **S**
5. A turtle's shell has many spots. — **S**
6. Anna took pictures of two raccoons' dens. — **P**

Complete each sentence with the singular possessive form of the noun in the parentheses.

1. Jim wanted to play basketball at **Carol's** house. (Carol)
2. One of **Jim's** new sneakers was missing. (Jim)
3. He looked under his **sister's** desk. (sister)
4. He crawled under his **brother's** bed to look. (brother)
5. It was outside in his **dad's** flower garden. (dad)
6. Jim saw his **dog's** footprints in the dirt. (dog)

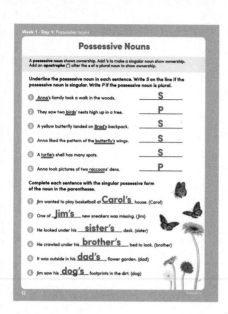

12

The Short List

Use the lines below to make a list of words with short /a/, /e/, /i/, /o/, and /u/. Choose words from the Word Bank.

Word Bank

bag	beg	bit	bog	dam
gas	gum	let	lip	met
box	mud	not	nut	pig

Short /a/	**bag**	**dam**	**gas**
Short /e/	**beg**	**let**	**met**
Short /i/	**bit**	**lip**	**pig**
Short /o/	**box**	**not**	**bog**
Short /u/	**gum**	**mud**	**nut**

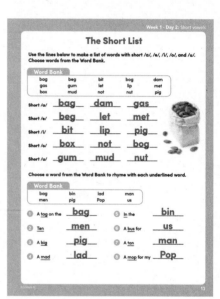

Choose a word from the Word Bank to rhyme with each underlined word.

Word Bank

bag	bin	lad	man
men	pig	Pop	us

1. A tag on the **bag**
2. Ten **men**
3. A big **pig**
4. A mad **lad**
5. In the **bin**
6. A bus for **us**
7. A tan **man**
8. A mop for my **Pop**

13

A Whale of a Sentence

> A **statement**, or telling sentence, ends with a period (.).

Rewrite the sentences using capital letters and periods.

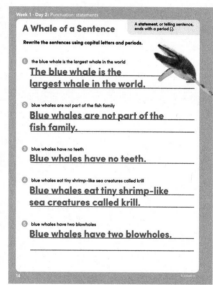

1. the blue whale is the largest whale in the world
   The blue whale is the largest whale in the world.

2. blue whales are not part of the fish family
   Blue whales are not part of the fish family.

3. blue whales have no teeth
   Blue whales have no teeth.

4. blue whales eat tiny shrimp-like sea creatures called krill
   Blue whales eat tiny shrimp-like sea creatures called krill.

5. blue whales have two blowholes
   Blue whales have two blowholes.

14

Who Did It?

> A **noun**, or naming part of a sentence can be a person.

Use the pictures to find naming parts to make each sentence complete. The first one is done for you.

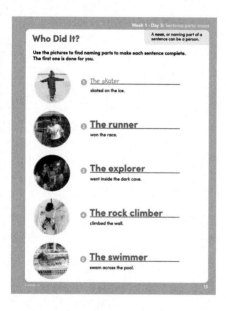

1. The skater skated on the ice.
2. **The runner** won the race.
3. **The explorer** went inside the dark cave.
4. **The rock climber** climbed the wall.
5. **The swimmer** swam across the pool.

15

Skip Counting Caterpillars

Each of these caterpillars is skip counting by a different number. Can you figure out what each one is counting by? Fill in the numbers that they have missed.

4 8 **16** 20 24 28 32 **36** 40

6 **12** 18 24 **30** 36 42 **48** 54 60

7 **14** 21 **28** 35 **42** 49 56 **63** 70

9 **18** 27 **36** 45 54 **63** 72 **81** 90

8 16 **24** 32 **40** 48 56 **64** 72 80

16

Send in the Subs

A **pronoun** is a word that can take the place of a noun.

Pronoun Substitutes

he   you   we   they   it   she

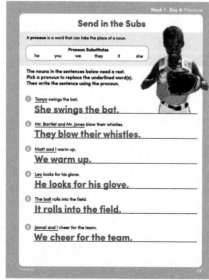

The nouns in the sentences below need a rest. Pick a pronoun to replace the underlined word(s). Then write the sentence using the pronoun.

1. Tanya swings the bat.
   She swings the bat.

2. Mr. Bartlet and Mr. Jones blow their whistles.
   They blow their whistles.

3. Matt and I warm up.
   We warm up.

4. Leo looks for his glove.
   He looks for his glove.

5. The ball rolls into the field.
   It rolls into the field.

6. Jamal and I cheer for the team.
   We cheer for the team.

17

Frog in the Bog

Help! Frances the Frog is lost in the bog. Help her find her way home. Move one box at a time in any direction except diagonally. She can only hop on boxes that contain even numbers. And, of course, she doesn't want to stop on a box already occupied by a hungry alligator. Draw a line to show her path!

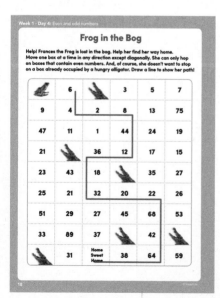

	6		3	5	7
9	4	2	8	13	75
47	11	1	44	24	19
21		36	12	17	15
23	43	18	8	35	27
25	21	32	20	22	26
51	29	27	45	68	53
33	89	37		42	
	31	Home Sweet Home	38	64	59

18

Courtney's Father

Read the story and answer the questions.

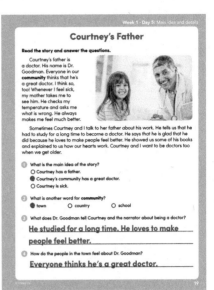

Courtney's father is a doctor. His name is Dr. Goodman. Everyone in our **community** thinks that he's a great doctor. I think so, too! Whenever I feel sick, my mother takes me to see him. He checks my temperature and asks me what is wrong. He always makes me feel much better.

Sometimes Courtney and I talk to her father about his work. He tells us that he had to study for a long time to become a doctor. He says that he is glad that he did because he loves to make people feel better. He showed us some of his books and explained to us how our hearts work. Courtney and I want to be doctors too when we get older.

① What is the main idea of the story?
○ Courtney has a father.
● Courtney's community has a great doctor.
○ Courtney is sick.

② What is another word for **community**?
● town ○ country ○ school

③ What does Dr. Goodman tell Courtney and the narrator about being a doctor?
He studied for a long time. He loves to make people feel better.

④ How do the people in the town feel about Dr. Goodman?
Everyone thinks he's a great doctor.

Sudoku Math

Every row, column, and 2-by-3 box should contain each of these digits in the answers: 1 2 3 4 5 6

Fill in each blank with the correct number to complete the fact.

7 − 6 = 1	15 − [3] = 12	10 − 5 = 5	13 − 7 = 6	8 − 4 = 4	9 − 7 = 2
[6] − 5 = 1	12 − 8 = 4	[2] − 5 = 7	11 − 6 = 5	9 − 6 = 3	[1] − 3 = 8
11 − 7 = 4	8 − 1 = 7	10 − [3] = 7	8 − 6 = 2	12 − 6 = 6	12 − 7 = 5
9 − [4] = 5	[2] − 7 = 5	[6] − 6 = 10	[4] − 9 = 5	6 − [1] = 5	[3] − 8 = 5
10 − 7 = 3	8 − 3 = 5	[4] − 7 = 7	[1] − 8 = 7	8 − [2] = 6	10 − 4 = 6
10 − 8 = 2	14 − 8 = 6	[1] − 5 = 6	1[3] − 8 = 5	7 − [5] = 2	10 − 6 = 4

Week 2

A Walk in the Park

> A **noun**, or the naming part of a sentence, can be a place or a thing.

Complete each sentence about the picture. Use the nouns in the Word Bank below.

Word Bank
bench   bridge   carousel   children   stream   swing

① The **swing** is near the tree.
② The **bench** is beside the slide.
③ The **children** are playing in the park.
④ The **carousel** has six sections.
⑤ The **bridge** is over the stream.
⑥ The **stream** runs through the park.

How Long Is It?

Use a ruler to measure each pencil. Measure from end to end. Write the measurement below.

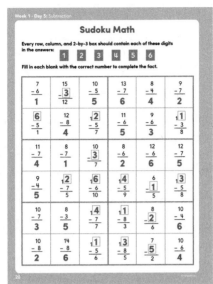

Ⓐ **2** inches
Ⓑ **2½** inches
Ⓒ **1½** inches
Ⓓ **2** inches
Ⓔ **3½** inches
Ⓕ **5** inches
Ⓖ **3** inches
Ⓗ **4** inches

Irregular Plurals

Most **plural nouns** end in **s**.

| 1 bird | 2 birds |

Irregular plural nouns don't just add **s** to the singular to become plural!

| 1 child | 2 children |

Irregular plural nouns change their spellings in different ways. Some don't change at all.

Mice are small rodents.
Geese are large birds that make a honking sound.
Sheep are animals whose fur is used for wool.
Male deer have antlers.

Word Bank
children   dresses   feet   leaves   teeth   wolves

Write the plural for each word below. Use a word from the Word Bank.
① tooth **teeth**
② child **children**
③ foot **feet**
④ dress **dresses**
⑤ leaf **leaves**
⑥ wolf **wolves**

Write the plural for each animal pictured below.
① **geese**
② **mice**
③ **sheep**
④ **deer**

Use a Number Line

Complete each equation. Use the number line below.

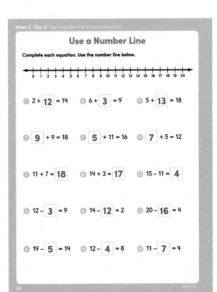

0 1 2 3 4 5 6 7 8 9 10 11 12 13 14 15 16 17 18 19 20

① 2 + **12** = 14   ⑥ 6 + **3** = 9   ⑪ 5 + **13** = 18
② **9** + 9 = 18   ⑦ **5** + 11 = 16   ⑫ **7** + 5 = 12
③ 11 + 7 = **18**   ⑧ 14 + 3 = **17**   ⑬ 15 − 11 = **4**
④ 12 − **3** = 9   ⑨ 14 − **12** = 2   ⑭ 20 − **16** = 4
⑤ 19 − **5** = 14   ⑩ 12 − **4** = 8   ⑮ 11 − **7** = 4

A Snail's Pace

Long-vowel sounds can be spelled in different ways. Some of the common spellings for long-vowel sounds are:

Long a	Long e	Long i	Long o
a_e	e_e	i_e	o_e
ai, ay	ea, ee	y, igh	oa, ow, oe

Read and write each word on the lines below. Then organize the words by their long-vowel sounds.

① deep
② hole
③ toe
④ ride
⑤ meal
⑥ fly
⑦ snail
⑧ blow
⑨ here
⑩ game
⑪ lay
⑫ goat
⑬ might
⑭ these

long-a sound	long-i sound
snail	ride
game	fly
lay	might

long-e sound	long-o sound
deep	hole
meal	toe
here	blow
these	goat

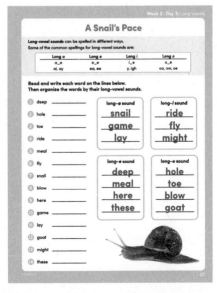

Prime Timer

Write the time 2 ways.   Example: 1:15   15 minutes after 1

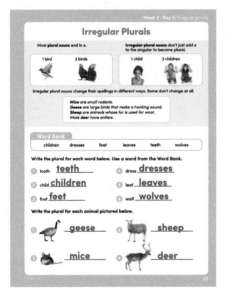

① **7:35**   **25** minutes to **8**
④ **3:50**   **10** minutes to **4**
② **9:15**   **15** minutes after **9**
⑤ **6:25**   **25** minutes after **6**
③ **9:55**   **5** minutes to **10**
⑥ **2:05**   **5** minutes after **2**

What's the Action?

The action part of a sentence is called a **verb**.
Example: *Chet walks to school every day.*

Look at each picture.
Then, complete each sentence about the picture using an action word, or verb.
Remember to use correct punctuation.

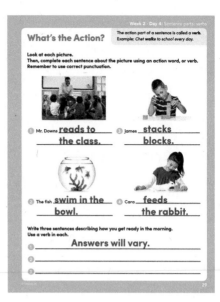

① Mr. Downs **reads to the class.**

③ James **stacks blocks.**

② The fish **swim in the bowl.**

④ Cara **feeds the rabbit.**

Write three sentences describing how you get ready in the morning.
Use a verb in each.

Answers will vary.

①
②
③

What does a teapot do when it is mad?

Add. Solve the riddle using your answers.

21 +14 **35** N	12 +15 **27** I	20 +19 **39** U	14 +14 **28** W	23 +31 **54** P	35 +13 **48** T
11 +13 **24** L	44 +12 **56** S	21 +43 **64** B	26 +21 **47** R	50 +18 **68** O	26 +53 **79** E

Solve the Riddle!

Write the letter that goes with each number.

I T   B L O W S
27 48   64 24 68 28 56

I T S   T O P
27 48 56   48 68 54

Abraham Lincoln

Read the article. Then answer the questions.

Abraham Lincoln was the 16th President of the United States. When he was a boy, his family lived in a small log **cabin**. It had one room and only one window. The walls were made from stacked-up tree logs. It had a dirt floor.

There was no electricity then. So, Abe's family got light from candles and the fireplace. Abe loved to read books by candlelight. One of his favorite books was about George Washington!

When Abraham Lincoln grew up, he became a lawyer. Then in 1861, he became President of the United States.

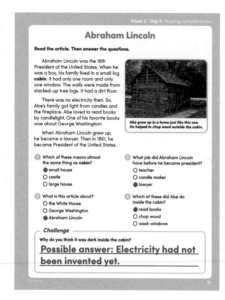

Abe grew up in a home just like this one. He helped to chop wood outside the cabin.

① Which of these means almost the same thing as **cabin**?
● small house
○ castle
○ large house

② What is this article about?
○ the White House
○ George Washington
● Abraham Lincoln

③ What job did Abraham Lincoln have before he became president?
○ teacher
○ candle maker
● lawyer

④ Which of these did Abe do inside the cabin?
● read books
○ chop wood
○ wash windows

Challenge

Why do you think it was dark inside the cabin?

Possible answer: Electricity had not been invented yet.

Parts of a Shape

Each shape has been divided into equal parts. Below each shape, write whether that shape is divided into two halves, three thirds, or four fourths.

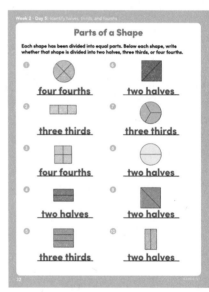

① four fourths
② three thirds
③ four fourths
④ two halves
⑤ three thirds

⑥ two halves
⑦ three thirds
⑧ two halves
⑨ two halves
⑩ two halves

Week 3

Adjectives

An **adjective** is a word that describes a person, place, or thing.

Read each sentence.
Write the adjective that describes the underlined noun.

① We live near a sparkling brook. — **sparkling**
② It has clear water. — **clear**
③ Large fish swim in the brook. — **large**
④ Busy squirrels play near the brook. — **busy**
⑤ You can enjoy breathing in the fresh air near the brook. — **fresh**

Complete each sentence by adding an adjective.

① I love **Answers will vary.** apples.
② I see a ___ ball.
③ I smell ___ flowers.
④ I hear ___ music.
⑤ I like ___ grapes.

Write three sentences that tell about the foods you like the best.
Use adjectives in your description.

Answers will vary.

Symbols of Comparison

Rewrite each statement. Use the symbols <, >, or =.
The first one is done for you.

① 5 is greater than 2
5 > 2

② 2 is less than 3
2 < 3

③ 8 is greater than 1
8 > 1

④ 19 is less than 23
19 < 23

⑤ 74 is greater than 73
74 > 73

⑥ 56 is equal to 56
56 = 56

⑦ 7 is equal to 7
7 = 7

⑧ 9 is less than 10
9 < 10

⑨ 5 is equal to 5
5 = 5

⑩ 98 is greater than 52
98 > 52

⑪ 200 is less than 201
200 < 201

⑫ 99 is less than 100
99 < 100

Lunch Lady
by Karen Jackson

Karen Jackson wrote about someone she admires. Read what she wrote.

I don't know her name. She is one of the workers in our school cafeteria. I call her Lunch Lady. She's my friend. There are many nice ladies in the cafeteria, but the Lunch Lady is the nicest of all. Every day she smiles at me when I go through the line. She says things like, "Hi Karen! Are you having a good day?" Lunch Lady always remembers that I like chicken nuggets the best and says, "Look, your favorite!" One day, I tripped and dropped my tray. Food went all over the floor. I was so embarrassed, but Lunch Lady came to my rescue. She helped me pick up the mess and she told me, "Don't worry about it. It's okay." That made me feel better. Another time, I was at the shoe store with my mom, and I saw Lunch Lady. She gave me a big hug. The reason I admire Lunch Lady is because she is friendly and kind.

Read each sentence below. Find the words that are wrong and cross them out.
Then above them write the correct word or words that make the sentence true.

① Karen wrote about Lunch ~~Man~~ **Lady**
② Karen's favorite food is ~~hot dogs~~ **chicken nuggets**
③ Lunch Lady ~~frowns~~ **smiles** when Karen comes through the line.
④ When Karen dropped her tray, ~~Miss Daniels~~ **Lunch Lady** helped her.
⑤ One time, Karen saw Lunch Lady at the ~~hardware~~ **shoe** store.
⑥ Karen admires Lunch Lady because she is friendly and ~~mean~~ **kind**.

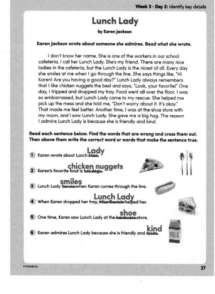

The Sign Snatcher

The sign snatcher has taken the plus and minus signs from each equation.
Can you put the correct ones back in?

Example:

15 ☐ 5 ☐ 1 = 11 → 15 − 5 + 1 = 11

Complete each equation. Put a plus or a minus sign in each of the boxes.

① 5 **+** 5 **+** 10 = 20
② 7 **+** 2 **+** 10 = 19
③ 8 **−** 3 **+** 5 = 10
④ 16 **−** 1 **−** 2 = 13
⑤ 100 **−** 100 **+** 50 = 50
⑥ 42 **+** 4 **+** 2 = 48
⑦ 78 **+** 2 **−** 10 = 70
⑧ 5 **−** 3 **+** 12 = 14

Remember to check your answers by trying the equations after putting in the signs.

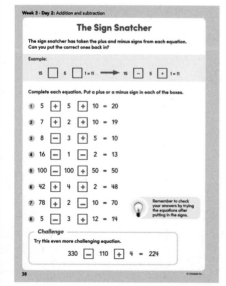

Challenge

Try this even more challenging equation.

330 **−** 110 **+** 4 = 224

Riddle Fun

Most verbs are regular. Their past-tense form ends in **-ed**.
Some verbs are **irregular**. The past-tense form of irregular verbs does not end in **-ed**.
The chart below shows the present and past tense of some irregular verbs.

Irregular Verbs					
Present Tense	eat	grow	ride	sit	tell	write
Past Tense	ate	grew	rode	sat	told	wrote

Read each riddle. Write the answer using
one of the past-tense verbs from the box.
Write a complete sentence.

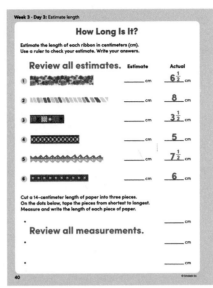

Possible answers shown.

1 I sat on the seat and pushed the pedals with my feet.
I went from my house to the park. What did I do?
__I rode my bike.__

2 I was shorter and weighed less last year.
My clothes were smaller, too. What did I do?
__I grew taller.__

3 I used my knife and fork.
Soon my plate was empty. What did I do?
__I ate dinner.__

4 I got out some paper and a pen.
I thought about what to tell my friend. What did I do?
__I wrote a letter.__

5 I took a seat and waited.
I stayed in the chair until it was my turn. What did I do?
__I sat down.__

© Scholastic Inc.   39

How Long Is It?

Estimate the length of each ribbon in centimeters (cm).
Use a ruler to check your estimate. Write your answers.

Review all estimates.

	Estimate	Actual
1	____ cm	$6\frac{1}{2}$ cm
2	____ cm	8 cm
3	____ cm	$3\frac{1}{2}$ cm
4	____ cm	5 cm
5	____ cm	$7\frac{1}{2}$ cm
6	____ cm	6 cm

Cut a 14-centimeter length of paper into three pieces.
On the dots below, tape the pieces from shortest to longest.
Measure and write the length of each piece of paper.

• ____ cm

Review all measurements.

• ____ cm

• ____ cm

40

Flex Yourself

A **pronoun** takes the place of a noun in a sentence. A **reflexive pronoun** is a special
kind of pronoun. Reflexive pronouns point back to the subject of the sentence.
Singular reflexive pronouns end in **-self**. Plural reflexive pronouns end in **-selves**.

Reflexive Pronouns	
Singular	**Plural**
myself	ourselves
yourself	yourselves
himself, herself, itself	themselves

Circle the reflexive pronoun in each sentence.
Then draw a line to the subject it points back to.
The first one is done for you.

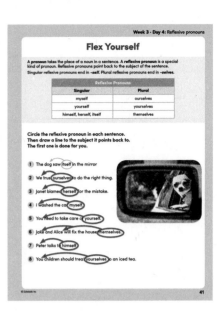

1 The dog saw itself in the mirror

2 We trust ourselves to do the right thing.

3 Janet blamed herself for the mistake.

4 I washed the car myself.

5 You need to take care of yourself.

6 Jake and Alice will fix the house themselves.

7 Peter talks to himself.

8 You children should treat yourselves to an iced tea.

© Scholastic Inc.   41

Add and Subtract

Above each number, write the number that is 10 more.
Below each number, write the number that is 10 less.
The first one is done for you.

	68			37			93
1	58	5		27	9		83
	48			17			73

	29			54			60
2	19	6		44	10		50
	9			34			40

	85			49			99
3	75	7		39	11		89
	65			29			79

	41			72			58
4	31	8		62	12		48
	21			52			38

42

Science Glossary

A glossary gives the meanings of difficult words in a book. Read the glossary
words below. Then fill in the bubbles for the words that mean the same as the
underlined words.

adaptation (ad-ap-TAY-shun) something that an animal has that helps it stay alive. A giraffe's long neck is an adaptation that helps it eat leaves high in trees.

coating (KOHT-ing) a layer that covers something

hail (hayl) balls of ice that fall from the sky

precipitation (prih-sip-ih-TAY-shun) water falling from the sky as rain, snow, hail, or sleet

shelter (SHEL-tur) a place where someone or something is safe and protected

survive (sur-VIV) to stay alive

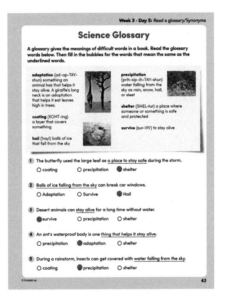

1 The butterfly used the large leaf as a place to stay safe during the storm.
○ coating   ○ precipitation   ● shelter

2 Balls of ice falling from the sky can break car windows.
○ Adaptation   ○ Survive   ● Hail

3 Desert animals can stay alive for a long time without water.
● survive   ○ precipitation   ○ shelter

4 An ant's waterproof body is one thing that helps it stay alive.
○ precipitation   ● adaptation   ○ shelter

5 During a rainstorm, insects can get covered with water falling from the sky.
○ coating   ● precipitation   ○ shelter

© Scholastic Inc.   43

Number-Pattern Parades

Figure out the pattern for each of these series.
What number comes next? Fill in the next number in the box at the end.

1 20 40 60 80 100 120 140 160 180   **200**

2 4 40 400 4,000 40,000   **400,000**

3 1 2 2 3 3 3 4 4 4 4   **5**

4 21 12 32 23 43 34 54   **45**

5 33 – 11 = 22   32 – 10 = 22   31 – 9 = 22   **30 – 8 = 22**

6 14 + 5 = 19   13 + 6 = 19   12 + 7 = 19   **11 + 8 = 19**

Challenge

What comes next in each of these patterns?

EXAMPLE: 3   1   4   2   5   3   6
      -2 +3 -2 +3 -2 +3

A 1   2   4   7   11   16   **22**

B 3   2   6   5   9   8   12   11   **15**

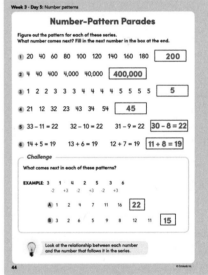 Look at the relationship between each number
and the number that follows it in the series.

44

Week 4

Adding Up Adverbs

An **adverb** is a word that tells how, when, or where an action takes place.

3	4	5	6	7	8	9	10	11	12	13	14	15	16	17	18	19	20
g	t	u	r	q	t	o	c	a	e	s	i	f	y	n	v	l

Add. Use the chart above to write letters on the blanks to spell adverbs.

g e n t l y
3+0 11+1 9+9 6+2 9+11 15+1

c l e v e r l y
1+9 17+3 6+1 9+9 6+2 4+2 18+2 5+11

q u i e t l y
5+2 4+1 7+7 6+2 14+2 18+2 14+2

c a u t i o u s l y
8+2 5+6 3+2 5+3 10+4 7+2 1+4 6+7 12+8 8+8

g r a c e f u l l y
2+1 3+3 9+2 4+5 8+7 15+1 15+5 11+9 9+7

Complete each sentence with an adverb from above.

1 The ballerina danced __gracefully__ to the music.

2 The children crossed the street __cautiously__

3 The cat __gently__ cleaned her new kittens.

4 The boy read his book __quietly__ at the library.

5 The detective __cleverly__ solved the mystery.

© Scholastic Inc.   47

Solving for Elapsed Time: Hours

Write the times shown on the left and on the right.
Then match each time on the left with the correct clock on the right.

LEFT   **RIGHT**

1 Fours hours after 6:00 = **10:00**   A = **4:00**

2 Two hours after 2:00 = **4:00**   B = **6:00**

3 Two hours before 2:00 = **12:00**   C = **10:00**

4 Seven hours after 1:00 = **8:00**   D = **12:00**

5 One hour before 7:00 = **6:00**   E = **8:00**

6 Six hours after 3:00 = **9:00**   F = **9:00**

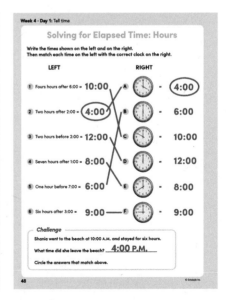

Challenge

Shania went to the beach at 10:00 A.M. and stayed for six hours.

What time did she leave the beach? **4:00 P.M.**

Circle the answers that match above.

48

Chugging Along

Write an ending for each sentence that tells where or when the action takes place.

Possible answers shown.

naming part	the action	where or when

1. The monkey | swings | in the trees.
2. The ball | flew | into the air.
3. Jenna's family | went | to the beach.
4. John | slept | on the sofa.
5. The glass | fell | on the floor.

© Scholastic Inc. 49

Use an Array to Add

Number each array of squares to find the total.
Then write an equation that shows the total as the sum of equal addends.
The first one is done for you.

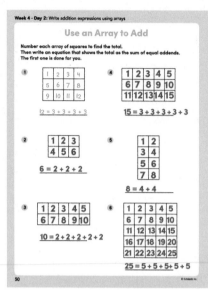

1.
```
1  2  3  4
5  6  7  8
9  10 11 12
```
12 = 3 + 3 + 3 + 3

4.
```
1  2  3  4  5
6  7  8  9  10
11 12 13 14 15
```
15 = 3 + 3 + 3 + 3 + 3

2.
```
1  2  3
4  5  6
```
6 = 2 + 2 + 2

5.
```
1  2
3  4
5  6
7  8
```
8 = 4 + 4

3.
```
1  2  3  4  5
6  7  8  9  10
```
10 = 2 + 2 + 2 + 2 + 2

6.
```
1  2  3  4  5
6  7  8  9  10
11 12 13 14 15
16 17 18 19 20
21 22 23 24 25
```
25 = 5 + 5 + 5 + 5 + 5

50

Ketchup and Mustard

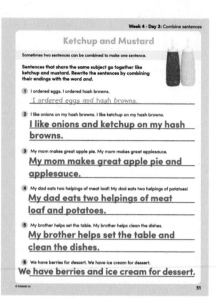

Sometimes two sentences can be combined to make one sentence.

Sentences that share the same subject go together like ketchup and mustard. Rewrite the sentences by combining their endings with the word *and*.

1. I ordered eggs. I ordered hash browns.
   I ordered eggs and hash browns.

2. I like onions on my hash browns. I like ketchup on my hash browns.
   I like onions and ketchup on my hash browns.

3. My mom makes great apple pie. My mom makes great applesauce.
   My mom makes great apple pie and applesauce.

4. My dad eats two helpings of meat loaf! My dad eats two helpings of potatoes!
   My dad eats two helpings of meat loaf and potatoes.

5. My brother helps set the table. My brother helps clean the dishes.
   My brother helps set the table and clean the dishes.

6. We have berries for dessert. We have ice cream for dessert.
   We have berries and ice cream for dessert.

© Scholastic Inc. 51

Measuring Up

Look at each picture. Estimate how long you think it is. Then measure each picture with a ruler. Write the actual length in centimeters.

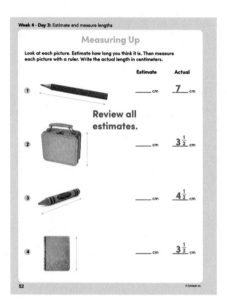

	Estimate	Actual

1. ____ cm | 7 cm

Review all estimates.

2. ____ cm | 3½ cm

3. ____ cm | 4½ cm

4. ____ cm | 3½ cm

52

Twinkle, Twinkle

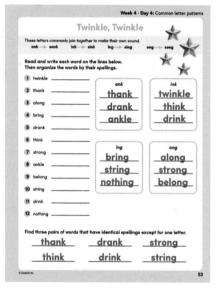

These letters commonly join together to make their own sound.
ank → sank   ink → sink   ing → sing   ong → song

Read and write each word on the lines below.
Then organize the words by their spellings.

1. twinkle ____
2. thank ____
3. along ____
4. bring ____
5. drank ____
6. think ____
7. strong ____
8. ankle ____
9. belong ____
10. string ____
11. drink ____
12. nothing ____

ank	ink
thank	twinkle
drank	think
ankle	drink

ing	ong
bring	along
string	strong
nothing	belong

Find three pairs of words that have identical spellings except for one letter.

thank	drank	strong
think	drink	string

© Scholastic Inc. 53

Expanding Numbers

Write each number in expanded form.
The first one is done for you.

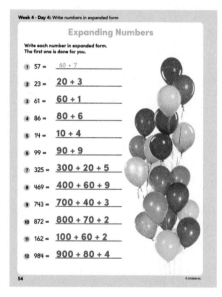

1. 57 = 50 + 7
2. 23 = 20 + 3
3. 61 = 60 + 1
4. 86 = 80 + 6
5. 14 = 10 + 4
6. 99 = 90 + 9
7. 325 = 300 + 20 + 5
8. 469 = 400 + 60 + 9
9. 743 = 700 + 40 + 3
10. 872 = 800 + 70 + 2
11. 162 = 100 + 60 + 2
12. 984 = 900 + 80 + 4

54

A Pencil Sandwich

Read the passage about how pencils are made.

How does the lead get inside a wooden pencil? Pencils are made out of strips of wood cut from cedar trees. Then, grooves are cut in the strips. A mixture of graphite and clay is laid into the grooves. (We call it lead, but it is really a graphite mixture.) Then another strip of wood is glued on top of the first one, making a pencil sandwich! The wood is rounded in rows on the top strip of wood and the bottom strip. Then the pencils are cut apart and painted. An eraser is added on the end and held in place by a metal ring. When you buy a pencil, you sharpen it, and then you are ready to write.

Now, look at the pictures and their descriptions. Number each picture in the order that a pencil is made as described in the passage.

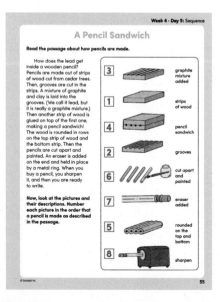

3 — graphite mixture added
1 — strips of wood
4 — pencil sandwich
2 — grooves
6 — cut apart and painted
7 — eraser added
5 — rounded on the top and bottom
8 — sharpen

© Scholastic Inc. 55

Nutty Math

Add. Then solve the riddle below using the code.

92	94	71	45	51	80	62
G	O	H	D	T	S	N

27 +18	55 +39	33 +47	69 +23	42 +29	47 +15	65 +15	22 +29	36 +16
45	94	80	92	71	62	80	51	52

What kind of nuts have no shell and nothing inside?

DOUGHNUTS

Add. Then solve the riddle below using the code.

55	64	34	71	28	50	82
N	L	A	S	U	W	T

21 +29	17 +17	38 +26	16 +39	19 + 9	56 +26	45 +26
50	34	64	55	28	82	71

What kind of nuts hang on the wall?

WALNUTS

56

Week 5

134

Page 1 — Short Vowels

Short Vowels

If a word has one vowel between two consonants, the vowel usually has a short sound.

Short Vowels:

| a in fan | e in hen | i in wig | o in cot | u in rug |

Say the name of each picture. Write the correct vowel to complete the word.

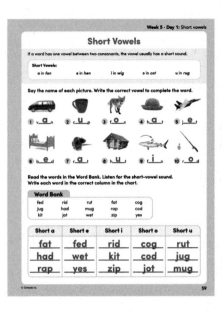

1. v_a_n
2. c_u_p
3. f_o_x
4. h_a_t
5. j_e_t
6. b_e_d
7. r_a_ft
8. h_u_t
9. f_i_sh
10. r_o_d

Read the words in the Word Bank. Listen for the short-vowel sound. Write each word in the correct column in the chart.

Word Bank

fed	rid	rut	fat	cog
jug	had	mug	rap	cod
kit	jot	wet	zip	yes

Short a	Short e	Short i	Short o	Short u
fat	fed	rid	cog	rut
had	wet	kit	cod	jug
rap	yes	zip	jot	mug

59

Page 2 — How Many Is That?

How Many Is That?

To solve these problems, you need to provide the numbers.
Read the clues, figure out the numbers, and solve the problems.

1. Multiply the number of states in the United States by the number of horns on a bull. What's the product? **100 (50x2=100)**

2. Subtract the number of bases on a baseball field from the number of letters in the alphabet. What's the difference? **22 (26−4=22)**

3. Add the number of days in most years to the number of seasons. What's the sum? **369 (365+4=369)**

4. Subtract the number of arms on an octopus from the number of sides on an octagon. What's the difference? **0 (8−8=0)**

5. Multiply the number of children in a set of twins by the number of wheels on a tricycle. What's the product? **6 (2x3=6)**

6. Subtract the number of eggs in a dozen from the number of hours in a day. What's the difference? **12 (24−12=12)**

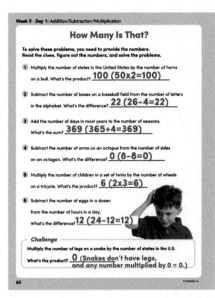

Challenge

Multiply the number of legs on a snake by the number of states in the U.S. What's the product? **0 (Snakes don't have legs, and any number multiplied by 0 = 0.)**

60

Page 3 — Silly Sentences

Silly Sentences

A sentence may have three parts: a naming part, an action, and a part that tells where or when.

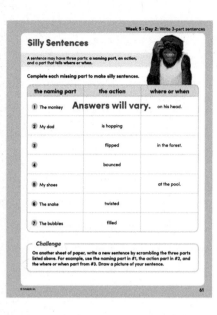

Complete each missing part to make silly sentences.

	the naming part	the action	where or when
1	The monkey	*Answers will vary.*	on his head.
2	My dad	is hopping	
3		flipped	in the forest.
4		bounced	
5	My shoes		at the pool.
6	The snake	twisted	
7	The bubbles	filled	

Challenge

On another sheet of paper, write a new sentence by scrambling the three parts listed above. For example, use the naming part #1, the action part #2, and the where or when part from #3. Draw a picture of your sentence.

61

Page 4 — Teenie Tiny Babies

Teenie Tiny Babies

Add or subtract.

U. 42 + 39 = 81
L. 53 − 48 = 5
N. 31 + 29 = 60
C. 74 − 28 = 46
O. 44 + 46 = 90

P. 75 − 37 = 38
H. 40 − 17 = 23
K. 27 + 36 = 63
S. 96 − 48 = 48
A. 62 − 48 = 14

G. 80 − 62 = 18
M. 55 + 16 = 71
R. 88 − 19 = 69

Write the letter that goes with each number.

I am smaller than your thumb when I'm born.
K A N G A R O O
63 14 12 14 69 90 90 90

I am even smaller.
K O A L A
63 90 14 12 90

I am smaller than a bumblebee.
O P O S S U M
90 38 90 48 48 81 71

Since we are so little, we live right next to our mother in a safe warm
P O U C H
38 90 81 46 23

62

Page 5 — At the Beach

At the Beach

A describing word makes a sentence more interesting.

Read the describing words on each beach ball.
Add the describing words to each sentence to make them more interesting.
Write each new sentence.

Possible answers shown.

1. The snow cone sat in the sun. (melting, bright)

   The melting snow cone sat in the bright sun.

2. Many children ran toward the ocean waves. (excited, crashing)

   Many excited children ran toward the crashing ocean waves.

3. My friends built a sand castle. (new, large)

   My new friends built a large sand castle.

4. Our dog tried to catch the beach ball. (playful, flying)

   Our playful dog tried to catch the flying beach ball.

63

Page 6 — Building a Boat

Building a Boat

The story is missing some words and numbers. Fill in the blanks with the number, noun, verb, adjective, or other type of word listed below the blank. Then solve the problem below.

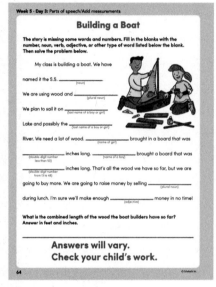

My class is building a boat. We have named it the S.S. _____ (noun). We are using wood and _____ (plural noun). We plan to sail it on _____ (last name of a boy or girl) Lake and possibly the _____ (last name of a boy or girl) River. We need a lot of wood. _____ (name of girl) brought in a board that was _____ (double-digit number less than 50) inches long. _____ (name of a boy) brought a board that was _____ (double-digit number from 15 to 45) inches long. That's all the wood we have so far, but we are going to buy more. We are going to raise money by selling _____ (plural noun) during lunch. I'm sure we'll make enough _____ (adjective) money in no time!

What is the combined length of the wood the boat builders have so far? Answer in feet and inches.

_____

Answers will vary. Check your child's work.

64

Page 7 — Cake and Ice Cream

Cake and Ice Cream

Two sentences that share the same subject can be combined to make one sentence by using the word *and*.

Rewrite the sentences by combining their endings.

1. The party was fun.
   The party was exciting.

   The party was fun and exciting.

2. We blew up orange balloons.
   We blew up green balloons.

   We blew up orange and green balloons.

3. We ate cake.
   We ate ice cream.

   We ate cake and ice cream.

4. The cake frosting was blue.
   The cake frosting was yellow.

   The cake frosting was blue and yellow.

5. We made a bookmark.
   We made a clay pot.

   We made a bookmark and a clay pot.

6. We brought games.
   We brought presents.

   We brought games and presents.

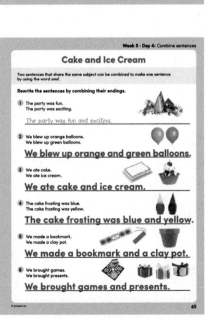

65

Page 8 — What do you call a swimmer...

What do you call a swimmer who was at the scene of a crime?

Subtract. Solve the riddle using your answers below.

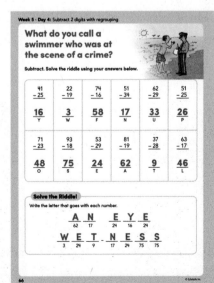

| 41 − 25 = 16 (Y) | 22 − 19 = 3 (W) | 74 − 16 = 58 (F) | 51 − 34 = 17 (N) | 62 − 29 = 33 (U) | 51 − 25 = 26 (P) |
| 71 − 23 = 48 (O) | 93 − 18 = 75 (S) | 53 − 29 = 24 (E) | 81 − 19 = 62 (A) | 37 − 28 = 9 (T) | 63 − 17 = 46 (L) |

Solve the Riddle!

Write the letter that goes with each number.

A N   E Y E
48 17   24 16 24

W E T N E S S
3 24   17 24 75 75

66

Page 9 — Curious Creature

Curious Creature

Read the story. Use details from the story to answer the questions below.

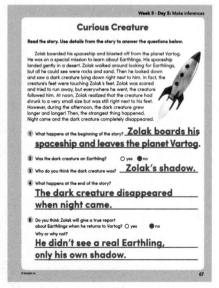

Zolak boarded his spaceship and blasted off from the planet Vartog. He was on a special mission to learn about Earthlings. His spaceship landed gently in a desert. Zolak walked around looking for Earthlings, but all he could see were rocks and sand. Then he looked down and saw a dark creature lying down right next to him. In fact, the creature's feet were touching Zolak's feet. Zolak was scared and tried to run away, but everywhere he went, the creature followed him. At noon, Zolak realized that the creature had shrunk to a very small size but was still right next to his feet. However, during the afternoon, the dark creature grew longer and longer! Then, the strangest thing happened. Night came and the dark creature completely disappeared.

1. What happens at the beginning of the story? **Zolak boards his spaceship and leaves the planet Vartog.**

2. Was the dark creature an Earthling? ○ yes ● no

3. Who do you think the dark creature was? **Zolak's shadow.**

4. What happens at the end of the story? **The dark creature disappeared when night came.**

5. Do you think Zolak will give a true report about Earthlings when he returns to Vartog? ○ yes ● no Why or why not? **He didn't see a real Earthling, only his own shadow.**

67

Compare Lengths: Centimeters

Use a ruler to measure the shapes below.
Record the length of each shape. Then find the difference.

Shape A
Shape B

Shape C
Shape D

① Length of Shape A: __3__ cm
Length of Shape B: __8__ cm
Difference: __5__ cm

② Length of Shape C: __5__ cm
Length of Shape D: __7__ cm
Difference: __2__ cm

Shape E
Shape F

Shape G
Shape H

③ Length of Shape E: __2__ cm
Length of Shape F: __5__ cm
Difference: __3__ cm

④ Length of Shape G: __6__ cm
Length of Shape H: __6__ cm
Difference: __0__ cm

Shape I
Shape J

⑤ Length of Shape I: __7__ cm
Length of Shape J: __15__ cm
Difference: __8__ cm

68

Week 6

The Cute Mule

The long-u sound can be spelled with the letters oo or u_e.

Read and write each word on the lines below.
Watch for a word that has an unexpected spelling.
Then organize the words by the letters that make the long-u sound.

① cute _____
② mule _____
③ tube _____
④ room _____
⑤ moon _____
⑥ rule _____
⑦ spoon _____
⑧ food _____
⑨ tune _____
⑩ who _____

oo	u_e
room	cute
moon	mule
spoon	tube
food	rule
	tune

unexpected spelling
who

Change one letter in each word below to spell a word from the activity above.

① cube **cute** or **tube**
② tube **tune**
③ spook **spoon**
④ male **mule**
⑤ role **rule**
⑥ why **who**
⑦ noon **moon**
⑧ zoom **room**
⑨ fool **food**

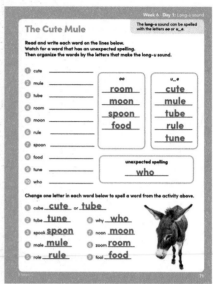

71

A Blowout Sale!

The store is having a sale! Circle the coins you would need to buy each item.
Circle the fewest number of coins possible.

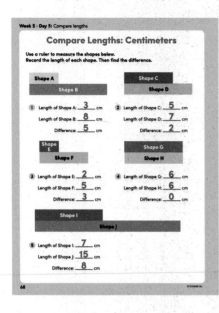

1 86¢
2 57¢
3 58¢
4 99¢

72

Hardworking Dogs

Read the article. Then answer the questions.

Many people serve in our armed forces. Some dogs do, too!

These dogs work hard, just like human soldiers. They are trained for a long time. They go where soldiers go, even when it's dangerous.

They help soldiers with different jobs. Dogs use their sense of smell to search for things. They help rescue people. They also protect soldiers.

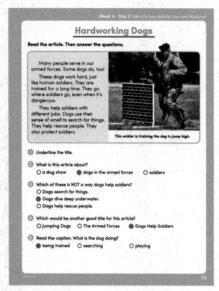

This soldier is training the dog to jump high.

① Underline the title.

② What is this article about?
○ a dog show ● dogs in the armed forces ○ soldiers

③ Which of these is NOT a way dogs help soldiers?
○ Dogs search for things.
● Dogs dive deep underwater.
○ Dogs help rescue people.

④ Which would be another good title for this article?
○ Jumping Dogs ○ The Armed Forces ● Dogs Help Soldiers

⑤ Read the caption. What is the dog doing?
● being trained ○ searching ○ playing

73

Measure the Shape

Use a ruler to measure in centimeters each line segment below.
Then record the data on the line plot. The first one is done for you.

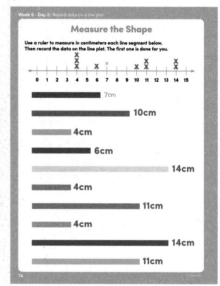

7cm
10cm
4cm
6cm
14cm
4cm
11cm
4cm
14cm
11cm

74

Ask Mother Goose

A sentence that asks a question ends with a **question mark (?)**.
It often begins with one of these words:
Who   What   Where   When   Why   Will   Could

Rewrite the questions using capital letters and question marks.

① where is the king's castle
Where is the king's castle?

② who helped Humpty Dumpty
Who helped Humpty Dumpty?

③ why did the cow jump over the moon
Why did the cow jump over the moon?

④ will the frog become a prince
Will the frog become a prince?

⑤ could the three mice see
Could the three mice see?

75

Who Dropped the Ice Cream?

Each of these words has a short-vowel spelling with one final consonant.
Before adding an ending such as -ing or -ed, double the final consonant.

Read and write each word on the lines below.
Underline the words with double consonants.
Then organize the words by their endings.

① drop _____
② dropped _____
③ beg _____
④ begged _____
⑤ skip _____
⑥ skipping _____
⑦ tap _____
⑧ tapping _____
⑨ run _____
⑩ running _____

no ending	-ed ending
drop	dropped
beg	begged
skip	
tap	-ing ending
run	skipping
	tapping
	running

Unscramble the letters to spell words from the activity above.

① nunigrn **running**
② propedd **dropped**
③ snigippk **skipping**
④ dgebge **begged**
⑤ ipsk **skip**
⑥ patnpig **tapping**

76

There Goes the Ball!

The letters **aw** make a sound in the word *law*. The letters **all** make the sound in the word *ball*.
These are two different sounds.

Read and write each word on the lines below.
Then organize the words by either aw or all.

① fall _____
② jaw _____
③ ball _____
④ hall _____
⑤ paw _____
⑥ saw _____
⑦ call _____
⑧ yawn _____
⑨ draw _____

aw	all
jaw	fall
paw	ball
saw	hall
yawn	call
draw	

Write a word from above that begins with the same letter as the picture.

① **saw**
② **fall**
③ **hall**
④ **jaw**
⑤ **call**
⑥ **paw**
⑦ **draw**
⑧ **ball**
⑨ **yawn**

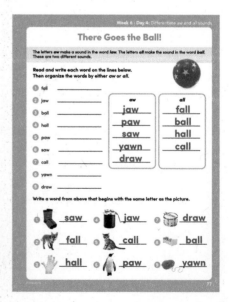

77

Cool Penguins

This penguin family is part of a winter parade. They need to line up by height. Give them a hand! Use a ruler to measure each penguin. Label each penguin with its height in centimeters.

Paul	Peter	Patty	Petunia
Height: 10½ cm	Height: 6½ cm	Height: 4½ cm	Height: 8½ cm

Write the name of each penguin in order of height, from the shortest to the tallest.

__Patty__ (shortest) __Peter__ __Petunia__ __Paul__ (tallest)

My Monster

Read the story.

I saw a scary monster that lived in a cave. It had shaggy fur and a long, striped tail. It had ugly, black teeth. Its three horns were shaped like arrows. Its nose was crooked. One of its feet was bigger than the other three. "Wake up! Time for breakfast," Mom said. Oh good! It was only a dream.

Read the directions below carefully. Follow the directions. Look for key words such as circle, underline, and color.

1. What did the monster's tail look like? Circle it.
2. What did the monster's teeth look like? Draw a box around them.
3. What did the monster's horns look like? Color them green.
4. What did the monster's nose look like? Underline it.
5. What did the monster's feet look like? Color them blue.
6. Which one of these is the correct picture of the monster? Draw a cave around it.

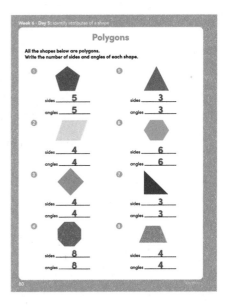

Polygons

All the shapes below are polygons.
Write the number of sides and angles of each shape.

1. sides 5, angles 5
2. sides 4, angles 4
3. sides 4, angles 4
4. sides 8, angles 8
5. sides 3, angles 3
6. sides 6, angles 6
7. sides 3, angles 3
8. sides 4, angles 4

Week 7

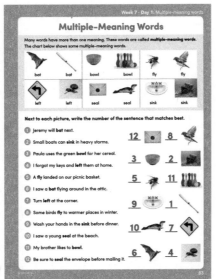

Multiple-Meaning Words

Many words have more than one meaning. These words are called **multiple-meaning words**. The chart below shows some multiple-meaning words.

bat | bat | bowl | bowl | fly | fly
left | left | seal | seal | sink | sink

Next to each picture, write the number of the sentence that matches best.

1. Jeremy will **bat** next. — 12, 8
2. Small boats can **sink** in heavy storms. — 3, 2
3. Paula uses the green **bowl** for her cereal. — 5, 11
4. I forgot my keys and **left** them at home. — 9, 1
5. A **fly** landed on our picnic basket. — 10, 7
6. I saw a **bat** flying around in the attic. — 6, 4
7. Turn **left** at the corner.
8. Some birds **fly** to warmer places in winter.
9. Wash your hands in the **sink** before dinner.
10. I saw a young **seal** at the beach.
11. My brother likes to **bowl**.
12. Be sure to **seal** the envelope before mailing it.

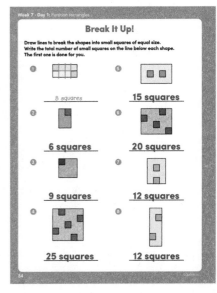

Break It Up!

Draw lines to break the shapes into small squares of equal size. Write the total number of small squares on the line below each shape. The first one is done for you.

1. 8 squares
2. 6 squares
3. 9 squares
4. 25 squares
5. 15 squares
6. 20 squares
7. 12 squares
8. 12 squares

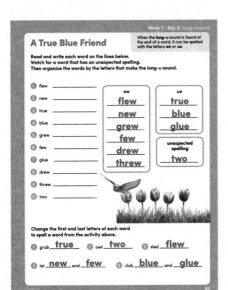

A True Blue Friend

When the **long-u** sound is found at the end of a word, it can be spelled with the letters *ew* or *ue*.

Read and write each word on the lines below. Watch for a word that has an unexpected spelling. Then organize the words by the letters that make the long-u sound.

1. flew
2. new
3. true
4. blue
5. grew
6. few
7. glue
8. drew
9. threw
10. two

ew	ue
flew	true
new	blue
grew	glue
few	**unexpected spelling**
drew	two
threw	

Change the first and last letters of each word to spell a word from the activity above.

1. grub __true__
2. owl __two__
3. sled __flew__
4. let __new__ and __few__
5. club __blue__ and __glue__

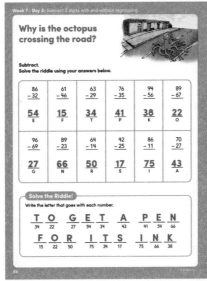

Why is the octopus crossing the road?

Subtract.
Solve the riddle using your answers below.

86 − 32	61 − 46	63 − 29	76 − 35	94 − 56	89 − 67
54 E	**15** F	**34** T	**41** P	**38** K	**22** O
96 − 69	89 − 23	64 − 14	42 − 25	86 − 11	70 − 27
27 G	**66** N	**50** R	**17** S	**75** I	**43** A

Solve the Riddle!
Write the letter that goes with each number.

T O G E T A P E N
34 22 27 54 34 43 41 54 66

F O R I T S I N K
15 22 50 75 34 17 75 66 38

Mystery Boxes

Describing words help you imagine how something looks, feels, smells, sounds, or tastes.

Read the describing words to guess the mystery object. Use the words in the Word Bank.

Word Bank
ball   bat   blanket   cracker

- soft, puffy, warm — I am a __blanket__
- hard, wood, long — I am a __bat__
- square, dry, crisp — I am a __cracker__
- round, bouncy, red — I am a __ball__

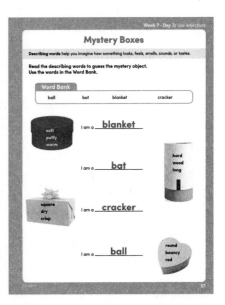

Add and Subtract

Above each number, write the number that is 100 more.
Below each number, write the number that is 100 less.
The first one is done for you.

	319		673		552	
①	219	⑤	573	⑨	452	
	119		473		352	
	309		599		423	
②	209	⑥	499	⑩	323	
	109		399		223	
	556		800		654	
③	456	⑦	700	⑪	554	
	356		600		454	
	333		708		917	
④	233	⑧	608	⑫	817	
	133		508		717	

Adding Words

A compound noun is made up of two smaller words put together.

Can you figure out what these compound nouns are?
Read the clues. Then write the compound noun.

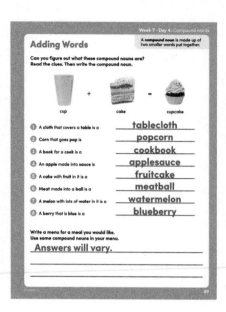

cup + cake = cupcake

① A cloth that covers a table is a ___ **tablecloth**
② Corn that goes pop is ___ **popcorn**
③ A book for a cook is a ___ **cookbook**
④ An apple made into sauce is ___ **applesauce**
⑤ A cake with fruit in it is a ___ **fruitcake**
⑥ Meat made into a ball is a ___ **meatball**
⑦ A melon with lots of water in it is a ___ **watermelon**
⑧ A berry that is blue is a ___ **blueberry**

Write a menu for a meal you would like.
Use some compound nouns in your menu.

Answers will vary.

Bamboo Graph

Bamboo is a super-plant. It can grow much taller than people. It can be as big as a tree. But bamboo is actually a kind of grass. The graph below shows how much a new bamboo plant grew over time. Use the graph to answer the questions.

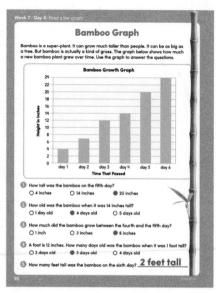

Bamboo Growth Graph

① How tall was the bamboo on the fifth day?
○ 4 inches ○ 14 inches ● 20 inches

② How old was the bamboo when it was 14 inches tall?
○ 1 day old ● 4 days old ○ 5 days old

③ How much did the bamboo grow between the fourth and the fifth day?
○ 1 inch ○ 3 inches ● 6 inches

④ A foot is 12 inches. How many days old was the bamboo when it was 1 foot tall?
○ 1 day old ● 3 days old ○ 4 days old

⑤ How many feet tall was the bamboo on the sixth day? **2 feet tall**

Did You Feed My Cow?

Read the poem aloud. Then underline the words that create rhythm in the poem.

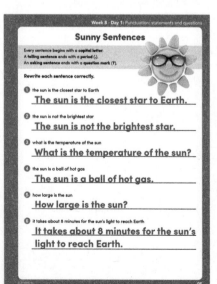

Did you feed my <u>cow</u>?
Yes, Ma'am!
Will you tell me <u>how</u>?
Yes, Ma'am!
Oh, what did you <u>give her</u>?
Corn and hay.
Oh, what did you <u>give her</u>?
Corn and hay.
Did you milk her <u>good</u>?
Yes, Ma'am!
Did you do like you <u>should</u>?
Yes, Ma'am!
<u>Oh, how did you milk her?</u>
<u>Swish! Swish! Swish!</u>
<u>Oh, how did you milk her?</u>
<u>Swish! Swish! Swish!</u>

Exact Change, Please

Read each amount on the left. Write the exact number of coins needed to exactly total the amount. There are many combinations you might make, but you must pick the fewest coins possible. The first one is done for you.

Example: You could make 33¢ with 3 dimes and 3 pennies, but this would take 6 coins. Using a quarter, a nickel, and 3 pennies uses just 5 coins.

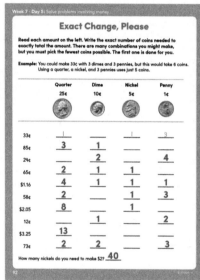

	Quarter 25¢	Dime 10¢	Nickel 5¢	Penny 1¢
33¢	1			3
85¢	3	1		
24¢		2		4
65¢	2	1	1	
$1.16	4	1		1
58¢	2		1	3
$2.05	8		1	
12¢		1		2
$3.25	13			
73¢	2	2		3

How many nickels do you need to make $2? **40**

Week 8

Sunny Sentences

Every sentence begins with a **capital letter**.
A **telling sentence** ends with a **period** (.).
An **asking sentence** ends with a **question mark** (?).

Rewrite each sentence correctly.

① the sun is the closest star to Earth
The sun is the closest star to Earth.

② the sun is not the brightest star
The sun is not the brightest star.

③ what is the temperature of the sun
What is the temperature of the sun?

④ the sun is a ball of hot gas
The sun is a ball of hot gas.

⑤ how large is the sun
How large is the sun?

⑥ it takes about 8 minutes for the sun's light to reach Earth
It takes about 8 minutes for the sun's light to reach Earth.

Greater, Less, or Equal?

Compare the numbers. Use the symbols <, >, or =.

① 300 > 261 ⑦ 398 > 396 ⑬ 221 = 221

② 205 < 612 ⑧ 499 > 137 ⑭ 824 > 823

③ 685 = 685 ⑨ 932 < 941 ⑮ 547 > 544

④ 744 > 477 ⑩ 357 = 357 ⑯ 871 > 817

⑤ 918 < 991 ⑪ 423 < 500 ⑰ 925 < 986

⑥ 154 < 211 ⑫ 599 < 603 ⑱ 613 < 761

Side by Side

A compound word is made up of two smaller words put together.

Complete the crossword puzzle with the missing part of each compound word. Use the Word Bank to help you.

Word Bank
ball, bath, brush, bed, cake, down, farm, finger, flower, ground, hive, knob, lid, plane, shelf, walk

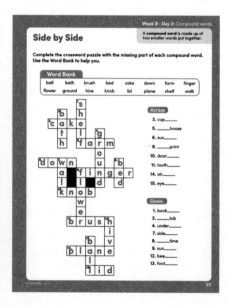

Across
3. cake
5. ___house
6. sun___
9. ___print
10. door___
11. tooth___
14. air___
15. eye___

Down
1. book___
2. ___tub
4. ___under
7. side___
9. sun___
12. bee___
13. foot___

138

Standard Numbers

Write each number in standard form.

1. 80 + 4 = __84__
2. 30 + 9 = __39__
3. 70 + 8 = __78__
4. 10 + 2 = __12__
5. 50 + 7 = __57__
6. 40 + 9 = __49__
7. 300 + 80 + 60 = __386__
8. 400 + 70 + 5 = __475__
9. 600 + 40 + 3 = __643__
10. 100 + 30 + 2 = __132__
11. 900 + 30 + 8 = __938__
12. 200 + 60 + 4 = __264__

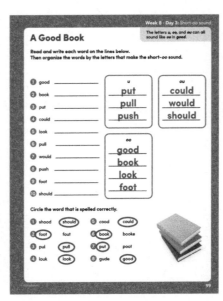
500 + 50 + 7 = 557

A Good Book

The letters u, oo, and ou can all sound like oo in good.

Read and write each word on the lines below.
Then organize the words by the letters that make the short-oo sound.

1. good _____
2. book _____
3. put _____
4. could _____
5. look _____
6. pull _____
7. would _____
8. push _____
9. foot _____
10. should _____

u	ou
put	could
pull	would
push	should

oo
good
book
look
foot

Circle the word that is spelled correctly.

1. shood (should)
2. (foot) fout
3. pul (pull)
4. louk (look)
5. cood (could)
6. (book) booke
7. (put) poot
8. gude (good)

What does Pinocchio feed his wooden dog?

Read the clocks. Write the times. Solve the riddle using your answers below.

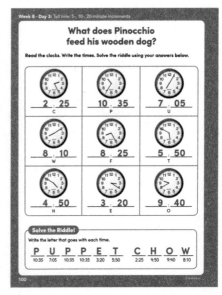

2:25 C
10:35 P
7:05 U

8:10 W
8:25 F
5:50 T

4:50 H
3:20 E
9:40 O

Solve the Riddle!

Write the letter that goes with each time.

P U P P E T   C H O W
10:35 7:05 10:35 10:35 3:20 5:50   2:25 4:50 9:40 8:10

Contraction Action

A **contraction** is a fast way to join words together.
One or more letters in the second word are left out and replaced by an apostrophe.
Example: **there is** becomes **there's**

Write the missing words or contractions.
The first one is done for you.

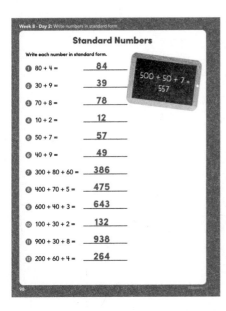

1. __was__ + not = wasn't
2. I + am = __I'm__
3. is + __not__ = isn't
4. here + is = __here's__
5. you + __are__ = you're
6. __does__ + not = doesn't
7. they + have = __they've__
8. we + will = __we'll__
9. should + __have__ = should've
10. let + us = __let's__
11. who + is = __who's__
12. you + would = __you'd__
13. who + __have__ = who've
14. we + are = __we're__

What happens once in every minute, twice in every moment, but not once in a hundred years?

Add. Solve the riddle using your answers below.

121 +124	322 +145	420 +166	104 +264	272 +302	131 +251
245 E	**467** N	**586** R	**368** T	**574** A	**382** O

211 +131	140 +413	210 +235	126 +131	310 +119	123 +141
342 L	**553** F	**445** D	**257** H	**429** H	**264** M

Solve the Riddle!

Write the letter that goes with each number.

T H E
368 429 245

L E T T E R   M
342 245 368 368 245 586   264

Splash Into Safety

Read the article. Then answer the questions below.

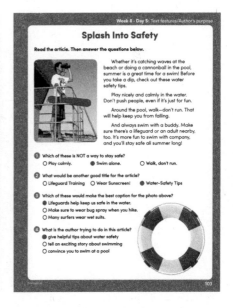

Whether it's catching waves at the beach or doing a cannonball in the pool, summer is a great time for a swim! Before you take a dip, check out these water safety tips.

Play nicely and calmly in the water. Don't push people, even if it's just for fun.

Around the pool, walk—don't run. That will help keep you from falling.

And always swim with a buddy. Make sure there's a lifeguard or an adult nearby, too. It's more fun to swim with company, and you'll stay safe all summer long!

1. Which of these is NOT a way to stay safe?
   ○ Play calmly.   ● Swim alone.   ○ Walk, don't run.

2. What would be another good title for the article?
   ○ Lifeguard Training   ○ Wear Sunscreen!   ● Water-Safety Tips

3. Which of these would make the best caption for the photo above?
   ● Lifeguards help keep us safe in the water.
   ○ Make sure to wear bug spray when you hike.
   ○ Many surfers wear wet suits.

4. What is the author trying to do in this article?
   ● give helpful tips about water safety
   ○ tell an exciting story about swimming
   ○ convince you to swim at a pool

Twin Test

These twins just took a math test. All the twins passed the test, but only one set of twins got all the answers right. To find out which, solve the addition problems under each child. The twins that got all the answers right have problems with the same answer. Circle the twins.

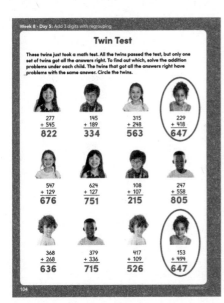

277 +545	145 +189	315 +248	229 +418
822	**334**	**563**	**(647)**

547 +129	624 +127	108 +107	247 +558
676	**751**	**215**	**805**

368 +268	379 +336	417 +109	153 +494
636	**715**	**526**	**(647)**

Week 9

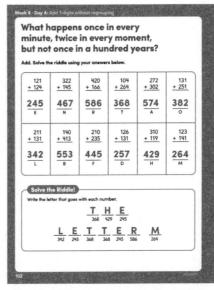

How Unusual!

The prefix **un-** means either "not" or "do the opposite of" the base of the word.

Circle each base word in the puzzle. The words go →, ↓, ↗, and ↘.
The first one is done for you.

Word Bank

unpack	untie	unload	unlock	unwind	undo
unknown	unfold	unable	unfair	unusual	unwise

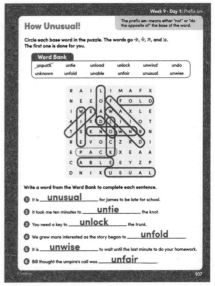

```
R A I L L I M A F X
N E E O F F O L D
I W E A W A X L E
A D I O D I G O T
T S K N O W N R N
R E V O C Z C E I
E P A C K X E A A
C A B L E S Y Z P
D N I K U S U A L
```

Write a word from the Word Bank to complete each sentence.

1. It is __unusual__ for James to be late for school.
2. It took me ten minutes to __untie__ the knot.
3. You need a key to __unlock__ the trunk.
4. We grew more interested as the story began to __unfold__.
5. It is __unwise__ to wait until the last minute to do your homework.
6. Bill thought the umpire's call was __unfair__.

Sandwich Shop

How much did each friend spend at the diner? Add to find out.

Menu

hot dog	$2.53	fruit salad	$2.90
blt	$2.49	veggies & dip	$2.84
turkey sub	$3.86	chips	$0.75
hamburger	$3.72	fries	$1.05
juice	$1.04	cupcake	$1.50
milk	$0.95	brownie	$1.95
shake	$2.17	cookies	$0.86

Sally
blt 2.49
chips .75
milk .95
brownie + 1.95
$6.14

Kamal
hamburger 3.72
fries 1.05
shake + 2.17
$6.94

Min
turkey sub 3.86
veggies & dip 2.84
juice 1.04
cupcake + 1.50
$9.24

Roberto
hot dog 2.53
fruit salad 2.90
brownie 1.95
juice + 1.04
$8.42

Michelle
turkey sub 3.86
chips .75
shake + 2.17
$6.78

Chet
blt 2.49
cookies .86
milk + .95
$4.30

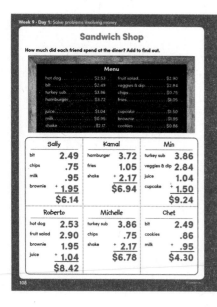

Vowel Digraph Outlaws

Vowel digraphs are two vowels, such as **ea**, that make one sound.
Usually the first vowel is long, and the second one is silent. For example:

ea words: **team** **leaf**	**ey** words: **monkey** **donkey**
ie words: **pie** **tied**	**ei** words: **ceiling** **protein**

But some words do not follow the rules. For example:

ea words: **bread** **early**	**ey** words: **obey** **prey**
ie words: **piece** **shield**	**ei** words: **height** **eight**

The underlined words in the sentences below have vowel digraphs that
do not follow the rules. What is the correct pronunciation of each word?
Next to each, write the letter of the picture that best illustrates the sentence.

1. This <u>steak</u> tastes <u>great</u>! **C**
2. Spread some jam on the <u>bread</u>. **E**
3. Trey said, "<u>Hey</u>, they won!" **D**
4. The police <u>chief</u> saw a <u>thief</u> stealing <u>pennies</u>. **A**
5. <u>Eight</u> <u>neighbors</u> rode in a <u>sleigh</u>. **B**

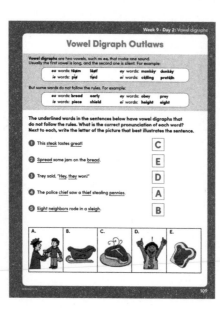

Why is the lion crossing the road?

Subtract.
Solve the riddle using your answers below.

424 − 121	299 − 107	576 − 130	698 − 541	379 − 101	867 − 125
303 E	**192** P	**446** R	**157** T	**278** A	**742** L

445 − 234	947 − 113	878 − 242	536 − 131	787 − 207	679 − 310
211 N	**834** G	**636** O	**405** D	**580** I	**369** H

Solve the Riddle!

Write the letter that goes with each number.

T O   G E T   T O   T H E
157 636   834 303 157   157 636   157 369 303

O T H E R   P R I D E
636 157 369 303 446   192 446 580 405 303

Zoo Reports

Compare means to look for things that are the same.
Contrast means to look for things that are different.

The second-grade class went to the zoo on a field trip. The next day,
the teacher asked the children to write a report about what they learned.
Read the two reports below.

Ryan

What I Learned at the Zoo

I learned about the giant tortoise. They eat grasses, plants, and cacti. They can weigh up to 450 pounds. Some tortoises live to be over 100 years old! That's older than my grandpa!

The slowest-moving mammal is the three-toed sloth. It hangs from trees and eats fruit. Some sloths sleep more than 20 hours a day. What a lazy animal!

I thought the albino alligator was really cool. It wasn't green. It was completely white all over. It was born that way.

Jessica

What I Learned at the Zoo

The tallest animal on earth is the giraffe. It eats leaves from the tops of the trees. Giraffes come from Africa.

I learned about an albino alligator. It was white instead of green. The guide told us that it was born without the coloring of other alligators.

I saw an owl sleeping in a tree. Owls sleep in the daytime and hunt at night. When they sleep, they don't fall out of the tree because they have sharp claws that lock onto the branch.

Ryan and Jessica each wrote about three animals. Write the names of the animals they wrote about in the correct circles. In the center, where both circles overlap, write the name of the animal that they both wrote about.

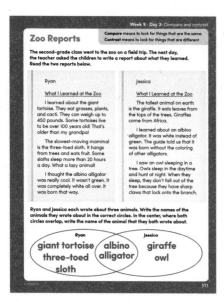

Ryan: giant tortoise, three-toed sloth
albino alligator
Jessica: giraffe, owl

Measurement Match-Ups

Measurements of Length
12 inches = 1 foot   36 inches = 1 yard   3 feet = 1 yard

Next to each measurement in the left column, write the letter
of the measurement in the right column that is equal in length.

1. 24 inches **d**   a. 6 inches
2. 6 feet **h**   b. 4 yards
3. 18 inches **g**   c. 9 feet
4. 36 inches **j**   d. 2 feet
5. 12 feet **b**   e. 4 feet
6. 60 inches **i**   f. $\frac{1}{3}$ foot
7. 4 inches **f**   g. $1\frac{1}{2}$ feet
8. 3 yards **c**   h. 2 yards
9. 48 inches **e**   i. 5 feet
10. $\frac{1}{2}$ foot **a**   j. 1 yard

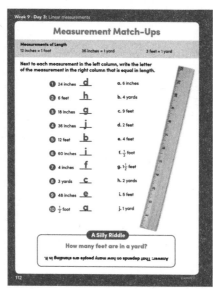

A Silly Riddle

How many feet are in a yard?

Answer: That depends on how many people are standing in it.

It Means . . .

Read each sentence.
Use the words in the sentence to figure out the meaning of the underlined word.
Circle the word or phrase that has a similar meaning to the underlined word.

1. This large vase will be ideal for that huge bunch of flowers.
   ready   (perfect)   ugly
2. If you do me this favor, I will be eternally thankful.
   quickly   sadly   (forever)
3. The strong motor propelled the boat quickly through the water.
   sunk   (pushed)   swam
4. Those two do not get along. They quarrel all the time.
   laugh   work   (argue)
5. I had not eaten all day and by night time I was ravenous.
   (starving)   tired   bored
6. While sitting in my chair, I elevated my feet onto the desk.
   (lifted)   washed   threw
7. These tickets are not valid anymore. You were supposed to have used them yesterday.
   torn   cheap   (good)
8. The artificial flowers were made of plastic.
   (fake)   real   red

Carnival Fun

Solve the problems below. Find your answers hidden in the carnival scene.
Circle each. Can you find all twelve answers?

15 33 + 27 = **75**	27 23 + 12 = **62**	34 23 + 34 = **91**	15 25 + 10 = **50**	16 14 + 14 = **44**	12 31 + 17 = **60**
28 22 + 45 = **95**	43 27 + 27 = **97**	10 17 + 18 = **45**	29 13 + 16 = **58**	37 31 + 17 = **85**	51 23 + 27 = **101**

Working Animals

Many animals work to help people. Some animals help rescue people.
Others help people with special needs.

Read the articles below. Then answer the questions.

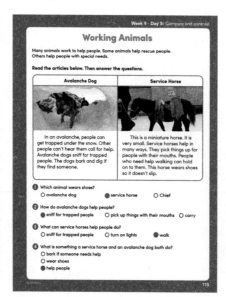

Avalanche Dog

In an avalanche, people can get trapped under the snow. Other people can't hear them call for help. Avalanche dogs sniff for trapped people. The dogs bark and dig if they find someone.

Service Horse

This is a miniature horse. It is very small. Service horses help in many ways. They pick things up for people with their mouths. People who need help walking can hold on to them. This horse wears shoes so it doesn't slip.

1. Which animal wears shoes?
   ○ avalanche dog   ● service horse   ○ Chief
2. How do avalanche dogs help people?
   ● sniff for trapped people   ○ pick up things with their mouths   ○ carry
3. What can service horses help people do?
   ○ sniff for trapped people   ○ turn on lights   ● walk
4. What is something a service horse and an avalanche dog both do?
   ○ bark if someone needs help
   ○ wear shoes
   ● help people

Compare Lengths

Use a ruler to measure the shapes below.
Record the length of each shape. Then find the difference.

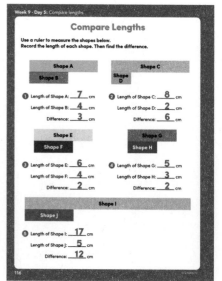

Shape A / Shape B
1. Length of Shape A: **7** cm
   Length of Shape B: **4** cm
   Difference: **3** cm

Shape C / Shape D
2. Length of Shape C: **8** cm
   Length of Shape D: **2** cm
   Difference: **6** cm

Shape E / Shape F
3. Length of Shape E: **6** cm
   Length of Shape F: **4** cm
   Difference: **2** cm

Shape G / Shape H
4. Length of Shape G: **5** cm
   Length of Shape H: **3** cm
   Difference: **2** cm

Shape I / Shape J
5. Length of Shape I: **17** cm
   Length of Shape J: **5** cm
   Difference: **12** cm

Week 10

Let's Do the Opposite

When the prefix *re-* is put at the beginning of the word *heat*, the word's new meaning is "to heat again." Here are some prefixes that mean "not" or "the opposite of."

dis-   in-   im-   un-

Read each description below. Write a new word on the lines that means the same. The new word should use the prefix *dis-*, *in-*, *im-* or *un-*.

1. not helpful — u n h e l p f u l
2. not patient — i m p a t i e n t
3. not tied — u n t i e d
4. not correct — i n c o r r e c t
5. not honest — d i s h o n e s t
6. not possible — i m p o s s i b l e
7. not agree — d i s a g r e e
8. not fair — u n f a i r

To find the answer to the question below, write the letter that goes with each number.

Where are a cricket's ears?

o n i t s f r o n t l e g s

What game do little monsters like to play?

Subtract.
Solve the riddle using your answers below.

748 − 437	574 − 419	133 + 129	317 + 487	738 − 218	629 + 298
311 F	**155** E	**262** S	**804** T	**520** I	**927** N
937 − 248	323 + 413	754 − 276	585 + 279	354 − 257	141 + 102
689 A	**736** H	**478** K	**864** D	**97** R	**243** M

Solve the Riddle!
Write the letter that goes with each number.

H I D E A N D
736 520 864   155 689 927 864

S H R I E K
262 736 97 520 155 478

The Outdoors

Synonyms are words that mean nearly the same thing.

Read each sentence.
Circle the word that means almost the same as the underlined word.

1. Tom was outside for just five minutes.
   after   (only)   over
2. Please save this seat for me.
   bring   buy   (keep)
3. The three bears lived in the woods.
   (forest)   house   tent
4. Pam went to bed because she was sleepy.
   quiet   (tired)   awake
5. First the cat sniffed the food, then she ate it.
   (smelled)   pulled   pushed
6. Mary tore her best dress.
   mended   (ripped)   broke
7. The teacher spoke in a soft voice.
   cheered   (talked)   screamed
8. I am glad that the flower has bloomed.
   angry   asking   (happy)

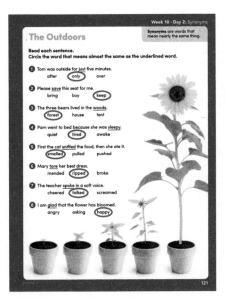

Seashells by the Seashore

Sally sees seashells by the seashore and collects them each summer. To learn how many seashells she has collected over the years, study the bar graph below.

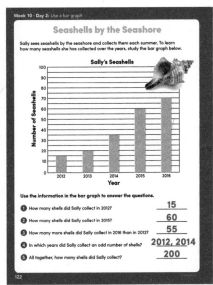

Sally's Seashells
(Number of Seashells vs. Year: 2012, 2013, 2014, 2015, 2016)

Use the information in the bar graph to answer the questions.

1. How many shells did Sally collect in 2012? — **15**
2. How many shells did Sally collect in 2015? — **60**
3. How many more shells did Sally collect in 2016 than in 2012? — **55**
4. In which years did Sally collect an odd number of shells? — **2012, 2014**
5. All together, how many shells did Sally collect? — **200**

Hunter

Read each sentence below.

Then Sarah brought Hunter home.

As Sarah walked down the street, a big dog ran towards her.

Then Sarah realized that she knew the dog.

Sarah hugged Hunter when he got to her.

Her face turned white with fear.

Its name was Hunter.

The sentences above tell a story but they are out of order. Rewrite the sentences in the correct order. Then read the story.

As Sarah walked down the street, a big dog ran towards her. Her face turned white with fear. Then Sarah realized that she knew the dog. Its name was Hunter. Sarah hugged Hunter when he got to her. Then Sarah brought Hunter home.

Animal Facts

Add or subtract.

T	O	L	P	A	W	I
247 + 253 = **500**	463 + 440 = **903**	139 + 146 = **285**	639 + 207 = **846**	391 + 144 = **535**	459 + 492 = **951**	198 + 672 = **870**

P	L	I	R	A	O	A
842 − 314 = **528**	504 + 475 = **979**	500 − 293 = **207**	457 + 364 = **821**	903 − 339 = **564**	107 + 147 = **254**	924 − 108 = **816**

N	N	R	H	A
700 − 427 = **273**	983 − 174 = **809**	703 − 186 = **517**	258 + 553 = **811**	357 + 537 = **894**

Move across each row. Write the letter from each box with the correct number of hundreds in the order in which they appear.

- 2 hundreds: I am a cat that likes to sleep 20 hours a day. — L I O N
- 5 hundreds: I have four toes on my front feet and three toes on my back feet. — T A P I R
- 8 hundreds: I am a fish with razor-sharp teeth. — P I R A N H A
- 9 hundreds: I can see well at night but cannot move my eyes. — O W L

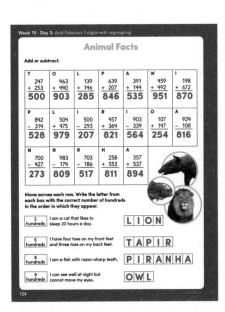

More Rule Breakers

In a **vowel digraph**, usually the first vowel is long and the second one is silent. However, in some words, both vowel sounds are heard. For example, you hear not one but two vowel sounds in *diet* and *neon*.

Read the words in the list below. Do you hear two vowel sounds? Draw a line from each word to the picture that matches it.

quiet
Brian
ruined
pliers
duet
fuel
science
lion

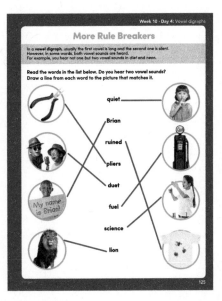

Food Frenzy!

Solve each word problem on the left and right. Draw a line to match each answer on the left with one on the right that is the same. (NOTE: Only the numbers have to match.)

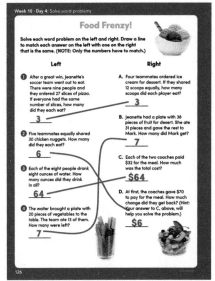

Left

1. After a great win, Jeanette's soccer team went out to eat. There were nine people and they ordered 27 slices of pizza. If everyone had the same number of slices, how many did they each eat? — **3**
2. Five teammates equally shared 30 chicken nuggets. How many did they each eat? — **6**
3. Each of the eight people drank eight ounces of water. How many ounces did they drink in all? — **64**
4. The waiter brought a plate with 20 pieces of vegetables to the table. The team ate 13 of them. How many were left? — **7**

Right

A. Four teammates ordered ice cream for dessert. If they shared 12 scoops equally, how many scoops did each player eat? — **3**
B. Jeanette had a plate with 38 pieces of fruit for dessert. She ate 31 pieces and gave the rest to Mark. How many did Mark get? — **7**
C. Each of the two coaches paid $32 for the meal. How much was the total cost? — **$64**
D. At first, the coaches gave $70 to pay for the meal. How much change did they get back? (Hint: Your answer to C, above, will help you solve the problem.) — **$6**

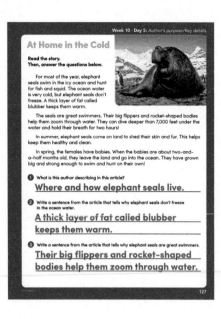

At Home in the Cold

Read the story.
Then, answer the questions below.

For most of the year, elephant seals swim in the icy ocean and hunt for fish and squid. The ocean water is very cold, but elephant seals don't freeze. A thick layer of fat called blubber keeps them warm.

The seals are great swimmers. Their big flippers and rocket-shaped bodies help them zoom through water. They can dive deeper than 7,000 feet under the water and hold their breath for two hours!

In summer, elephant seals come on land to shed their skin and fur. This helps keep them healthy and clean.

In spring, the females have babies. When the babies are about two-and-a-half months old, they leave the land and go into the ocean. They have grown big and strong enough to swim and hunt on their own!

❶ What is this author describing in this article?

__Where and how elephant seals live.__

❷ Write a sentence from the article that tells why elephant seals don't freeze in the ocean water.

__A thick layer of fat called blubber__
__keeps them warm.__

❸ Write a sentence from the article that tells why elephant seals are great swimmers.

__Their big flippers and rocket-shaped__
__bodies help them zoom through water.__

127

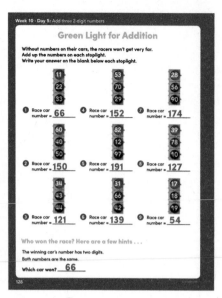

Green Light for Addition

Without numbers on their cars, the racers won't get very far.
Add up the numbers on each stoplight.
Write your answer on the blank below each stoplight.

❶ Race car number = **66** (11, 22, 33)

❷ Race car number = **150** (60, 40, 50)

❸ Race car number = **121** (34, 43, 44)

❹ Race car number = **152** (53, 70, 29)

❺ Race car number = **191** (82, 12, 97)

❻ Race car number = **139** (31, 66, 42)

❼ Race car number = **174** (28, 56, 90)

❽ Race car number = **127** (39, 78, 10)

❾ Race car number = **54** (17, 18, 19)

Who won the race? Here are a few hints . . .

The winning car's number has two digits.
Both numbers are the same.

Which car won? __66__

126

Photos ©: Getty Images: 21 (Artiga Photo), 29 girl feeding rabbit (Lane Oatey/Blue Jean Images); iStockphoto: 3sbworld, 5second, adekvat, adogslifephoto, adventtr, akhajon, Amy_Lv , AnaBGD, andresr, Andrew Rich, Andy Dean, Anna Kucherova, annebaek, Antagain, antpkr, BraunS, Brostock, byllwill, CareyHope, carlosalvarez, cbpix, chargerv8, Charles Mann, Christopher Futcher, cj2a, ClausAlwinVogel, clintscholz, clu, Cory Thoman, Craig Dingle, cynoclub, Daniel R. Burch, Daniya Melnikova, Danny Hooks, DawnPoland, desifoto, Diana Taliun, Diane Labombarbe, Eric Isselée, eurobanks, fmajor, gchutka, German, GlobalP, goir, HANA76, HEMARAT, Hong Li, huePhotography, iodrakon, jaroon, Jason Lugo, juliannafunk, juliedeshaies, Kais Tolmats, kali9, Kelly Richardson, Kenneth Wiedemann, Kharichkina, kiankhoon, Kitsune06, koosen, koya79, kyoshino, Lalocracio, lamiquela, larioslake, Lisa Thornberg, LucianoBibulich, Mac99, Marina Maslennikova, marioaguilar, matejmm, mehmettorlak, Michael Gray, Michael Guttman, Michael Phillips, MichaelStubblefield, MicroStockHub, migin, Mike Rickword, milehightraveler, Milkos, mipan, mjf795, monkeybusinessimages, MosayMay, Nastco, oksix, Omer Yurdakul Gundogdu, ozenli, Paffy69, pamela_d_mcadams, panda3800, Paolo Cipriani, peangdao, phasinphoto, PhotographerOlympus, pixhook, Ramone, RapidEye, rasslava, REM118, Robert Kirk, rusm, S-S-S, Sandra van der Steen, selimaksan, shapecharge, SimonKr d.o.o., sinankocaslan, stanley45, Steve Debenport, subjug, sunstock, svengine, tanuha2001, TheCrimsonMonkey, Tom Young, tomograf, Tomwang112, unalozmen, valio84sl, Vinicius Ramalh Tupinamba, vladru, Yayasya, zentilia; Shutterstock, Inc.: 126 vegetables (Africa Studio), 110 tapir (Anan Kaewkhammul), 72 doll (Andrey Osipets), 105 (berna namoglu), 37 hot dog (Christopher Elwell), 37 pizza slice (DenisNata), 65 party favors (digieye), 25 single bird (Eric Isselee), 25 sheep, 83 bird (Eric Isselee), 89 cake (Everything), 15 girl and boy in cave (Fanfo), 24 F & H pencils (GongTo), 38, 44 (haveseen), 37 milk (Hurst Photo), 52 lunch box (Hurst Photo), 125 pliers (Igor Pshenin), 52 notebook (imnoom), 125 gas pump (James Steidl), 89 cupcake (JFunk), 65 clay pot (Kitch Bain), 52 crayon (Lucie Lang), 126 fruit salad (M. Unal Ozmen), 18 alligator (Mammut Vision), 37 sandwich (margouillat photo), cover, 1 (Max Topchii), 15 boy ice skating (Nadezhda1906), 59 hat (onair), 15 boy in marathon (Peter Weber), 125 shirt (Picsfive), 65 gift boxes (Quang Ho), 77 ball (Richard Peterson), 65 bookmark (Robert Adrian Hillman), 24 C pencil (Ruslan Ivantsov), 72 chewing gum (Sergiy Kuzmin), 108 (stockphoto-graf), 15 boy swimming (Suzanne Tucker), 65 board game (Tatik22), 24 D & G pencils (urfin), 125 girl making quiet gesture (varandah), 52 pencil (wacpan), 28, 100 (Yuri Samsonov); Thinkstock: Andrey_Kuzmin, Artem Povarov, DCorn, ebrind, exopixel, Farinosa, Jupiterimages, Le Do, Tsekhmister, Zedcor Wholly Owned. **Illustrations:** by Janet Ambrust, Teresa Anderko, Anne Kennedy, Kathy Marlin, Mark Mason, Mike Moran, Sherry Neidigh, Carol Tiernon, and Bari Weissman.

FOR OUTSTANDING ACHIEVEMENT

CONGRATULATIONS!

This certificate is awarded to

I'm proud of you!